New York – 5/1/97

Essentials of Hindi Grammar

Murli Dhar Srivastava

Essentials of Hindi Grammar

a practical guide
to the mastery of Hindi

PASSPORT BOOKS
a division of *NTC Publishing Group*
Lincolnwood, Illinois USA

Titles Available in This Series:

Essentials of English Grammar
Essentials of Hindi Grammar
Essentials of Latin Grammar
Essentials of Russian Grammar
Essentials of Swedish Grammar
French Verbs and Essentials of Grammar
German Verbs and Essentials of Grammar
Italian Verbs and Essentials of Grammar
Japanese Verbs and Essentials of Grammar
Spanish Verbs and Essentials of Grammar

This edition first published in 1995 by Passport Books,
a division of NTC Publishing Group, 4255 West Touhy Avenue,
Lincolnwood (Chicago), Illinois 60646-1975 U.S.A.

Manufactured in the United States of America.

4 5 6 7 8 9 0 VP 9 8 7 6 5 4 3 2 1

PREFACE

Essentials of Hindi Grammar presents the major concepts of Hindi, the official language of India and the third most widely spoken language in the world. For ease of use, this book has been divided into 20 chapters, grouped into 5 sections. In each of these chapters, a specific grammar topic, such as gender, person, number, or case, is discussed, thus promoting quick and easy access to information.

Grammar explanations have been kept brief and to the point, allowing the largest amount of useful information to be covered. Examples drawn from everyday usage illustrate the rules presented, so that grammar is seen in the context of its real use. The examples used to illustrate grammar concepts were chosen for their authenticity—to represent the structures most frequently encountered in Hindi speech and writing. Thus, in addition to learning the fundamental rules of language, users will also acquire a familiarity with the style and vocabulary characteristic of modern Hindi.

Recognizing that correct pronunciation in a foreign language is a difficult task, the author has treated the topics of pronunciation and accent in depth. Some technical terms of Hindi grammar are also given with their English equivalents, since familiarity with the English terms may aid learning. A list of Hindi grammatical terms and their English translations may be found at the back of the book.

Essentials of Hindi Grammar is a thorough handbook that lends itself to a variety of uses. Because its basic approach is to provide simple, concise explanations, it can be used by students of varying levels, as well as by those who need a convenient reference to consult on confusing points of grammar. This book can be used for study and review, for individual or group work, as a part of a refresher course, or for business, travel, or research.

Essentials of Hindi Grammar is a unique and effective language tool. Its author and the publisher are confident that this comprehensive reference will prove indispensable to all those studying and teaching the Hindi language.

CONTENTS

Section I.

Section II.

Section III.

Section IV.

ABBREVIATIONS

Adj.	—	Adjective	Imp.	—	Imperative
Mas.	—	Masculine	Perf.	—	Perfect
Fem.	—	Feminine	Imperf.	—	Imperfect
Sing.	—	Singular	Pers.	—	Person
Plur.	—	Plural	Skt.	—	Sanskṛt
Tran.	—	Transitive	√	—	Sign of verbal root
Intrans.	—	Intransitive			

Transliteration in Roman Script

अ a आ ā इ i ई ī उ u ऊ ū ए e ऐ ai ओ o औ au ऋ ṛ

क् k	ख् kh	ग् g	घ् gh	ङ् ṅ
च् c	छ् ch	ज् j	झ् jh	ञ् ñ
ट् ṭ	ठ् ṭh	ड् ḍ	ढ् ḍh	ण् ṇ
ड़् ṛ	ढ़् ḍh			
त् t	थ् th	द् d	ध् dh	न् n
प् p	फ् ph	ब् b	भ् bh	म् m
य् y	र् r	ल् l	व् v	
श् ś	ष् ṣ	स् s	ह् h	

SECTION I

ĀGARĪ ALPHABET, WORDS IN HINDĪ, GENDER, NUMBER, PERSON, CASE AND CASE-SIGNS, PRONOUN AND ADJECTIVE

CHAPTER I

The Nāgarī Alphabet

Hindī is written in Nāgarī Script, which is a slightly modified form of Devanāgarī Script, the Script of the Sanskṛt language.

Hindī language has 11 vowels (स्वर) and 35 consonants (व्यंजन).

Vowels—There are two kinds of vowels—Short (ह्रस्व) and Long (दीर्घ)—

Short (ह्रस्व)		Long (दीर्घ)	
a.	अ	ā.	आ
i.	इ	ī.	ई
u.	उ	ū.	ऊ
ṛ.	ऋ	×	
e.	ए	a i	ऐ
o.	ओ	a u	औ

Consonants.

35.	k.	क्	kh.	ख्	g.	ग्	gh.	घ्	ṅ.	ङ्
	c.	च्	ch.	छ्	j.	ज्	jh.	झ्	ñ.	ञ्

It is better to use Nāgarī for the Hindī script and Devanāgarī for the Sanskṛt script. The Hindī script (Nāgarī) has omitted some letters as ॠ ॡ and added new letters as ड़ ढ़ and a new sign like (.) which is put below as ज़ फ़ etc.

Nāgarī (' of the city') is derived according to some from Nagar and according to others from Nāgar. Devanāgarī is nāgarī of the gods or of Devanagar. Devanagar is the 'city of gods' Nāgarī is used generally for the script and sometimes for the Hindī language also. See the use of Nāgarī in "Nāgarī Prachāriṇī Sabhā", Kāśī, a premier institution of Hindī.

ṭ.	ट्	ṭh.	ठ्	ḍ.	ड्	ḍh.	ढ्	ṇ	ण्	
t.	त्	th.	थ्	d.	द्	dh.	ध्	n	न्	
p.	प्	ph.	फ्	b.	ब्	bh.	भ्	m.	म्	
ṙ.	ड़	ṙh.	ढ़्	Two new consonants.						
y.	य्	r.	र्	l.	ल्	v.	व्			Semi-vowels.
ś.	श्	ṣ.	ष्	s.	स्					Sibilants.
h.	ह्									Aspirate.

Thus the Nāgarī alphabet has 11 vowels, 25 consonants, 2 new consonants, 4 semi-vowels, 3 sibilants and 1 aspirate.

The consonants cannot be pronounced without the help of vowel अ, (which is called inherent or 'Lupta' अ). So, often these क ख ग घ etc. are shown as क=क्+अ, ख=ख्+अ and so on.

Signs : There are some signs also which should be noted here. Their use and pronunciation will be dealt later.

: (h) Visarga—It is placed after a vowel as दुः in दुःख

ं Anusvār—It is placed above a letter—कं in कंठ

ँ Chandravindu—It is placed above a letter—रँ in रँगीला

् Hal—It is put below a letter—त् in सत्

New Signs.

(़) A point is put below letters क़, ख़, ग़, ज़, फ़, in some words of Arabic and Persian origin ज़ and फ़ are required to write several English words as Zone and Fat.

(ॅ) This sign is generally used to write English words in Hindī to represent the sound of 0 in 'boy' or 'college' as बॉय, कॉलेज

There is no sign to denote short ए and ओ though quite a large number of words in Hindī has this sound. For example एक्का, महतर, महता, महरा, नहरू, ओसारा, ओसाना, सोहागा, पराई।

In my opinion (ॆ ॊ) signs should be adopted for this purpose.

Some of these letters have optional forms also.

अ—अ, झ—झ, ण—ण, ल—ल।

There is another sign in Sanskṛt called Avagraha, which is used to denote the elision of an initial अ of a word, when it follows the vowel. Thus आज्ञा अनुसार is written as आज्ञाऽनुसार. But modern writers ordinarily do not use this sign. It is however used in Bhojpuri, a dialect, to give stress to अ sound चलऽभइया।

Representation of Vowels when added to Consonants

The full form of a vowel is used only when a word begins with a vowel or a vowel follows another vowel. When combined with a consonant it takes a special form which is called Mātrā by Hindī grammarians. अ has no written sign. The consonant itself implies a following अ. Thus the consonant क is really K-a and ख is Kh-a and so on. When a consonant simply, without the inherent अ, is to be denoted, a sign (्) is put below—(क् ख्). When a vowel in full form follows a consonant, it should be taken that the inherent अ is present in the preceding consonant—गई is ga + ī but ग् + ई is गी gī.

The sign of आ (ा) is written by a perpendicular stroke after a consonant, as का. The sign of इ is written by perpendicular stroke before a consonant and is connected by the sign of a hook above the upper line (ि). The sign of ई is written by a perpendicular stroke after a consonant and is connected by a hook on the right side above the upper line (ी). The sign of उ (ु) is indicated by a hook facing left attached to the lower end and the sign of ऊ (ू) by a hook facing right attached to the lower end of the consonant. The sign of उ and ऊ are attached in case of र in the middle of the consonant (रु रू). The sign of ऋ (ṛ) is indicated by a subjoined hook opening towards the right below (कृ). In ह however, this hook is attached in the middle (हृ). The sign of (ए) is a single stroke on the upper line (े) and of (ऐ) double strokes on the upper line (ै). The sign of ओ (ो) is a combination of a perpendicular stroke after the consonant and a single stroke on the upper line. The sign of औ is a combination of a perpendicular stroke after the consonant and double stroke on the upper line (ौ).

Signs of vowels combined with consonants.
Vowels added to क्

आ	ा	as	क्+आ=का
इ	ि	as	क्+इ =कि
ई	ी	as	क्+ई =की
उ	ु	as	क्+उ =कु
ऊ	ू	as	क्+ऊ =कू
ए	े	as	क्+ए =के
ऐ	ै	as	क्+ऐ =कै
ओ	ो	as	क्+ओ=को
औ	ौ	as	क्+औ=कौ

Combination of Consonants

When two consonants combine to form a conjunct letter (संयुक्ताक्षर) they omit some part of their original forms. Sometimes the preceding consonant only has to omit some part of its form and sometimes the following consonant and sometimes both consonants undergo some change in form. In some Sanskṛt words, three consonants combine to form a conjunct letter as (मत्स्य, माहात्म्य). Two letters are combined also by use of a Hal mark (्), but this is rarely done. Hal mark is used at the end of a Sanskṛt word only and should not be used with pure Hindī words.

As a general rule, the consonant which is pronounced first is put first in the conjunct form. Some are combined side by side (च्छ) ccha, while some adopt above and below arrangement (ट्ट) tta. In some cases the combined consonants adopt a disguised or independent form (त्त, त्र, ज्ञ). Some letters are arranged in both ways, that is side-by-side and above and below (क्क, क्क) as in पक्का, पक्का, (ल्ल, ल्ल) as in लल्ला, लल्ला (श्व, श्व) as in श्वान, श्वान, (श्च, श्च,) as in पुनश्च, पुनश्च

Examples of disguised or independent forms are :—

क्+त = क्त — मुक्त, Mukta

त्+त् = त्त — कुत्ता Kuttā.

क्ष, त्र, ज्ञ are really special conjunct forms of the following consonants क्ष=क्‌ ष्‌+अ, त्र=त्‌ र्‌+अ, ज्ञ=ज्‌ ञ्‌+अ

र takes different forms when it combines with a consonant.

(1). If र is pronounced before the following consonant, it is written above that consonant. It assumes the form of a hook opening to the right ॅ (र्म in धर्म). If it is followed by a consonant with a vowel whose Mātrā (vowel-mark) is above the upper line, it is written after the Mātrā, as in मूर्त्ति, सर्दी, मर्दों etc.

(2). If र follows a consonant having a vertical stroke, it assumes the form of a slightly slant stroke (्र) and is added below the consonant on its left side चक्र, ग्राम, वज्र .

(3). Before ट ठ ड ढ it assumes the form ^ which is added below राष्ट्र, पुण्ड्र (such words are generally Sanskṛt). ङ छ ट ड and ह retain their forms and the consonants combining with them are written below without the upper line :

अङ्कुर, उच्छ्‌वास, मट्टी, लट्ठा, हड्डी, प्रह्लाद .

य and म when combine with a preceding consonant assume the following special forms.

ह्‌+य=ह्य (बाह्य, ह्‌+म=ह्म, ब्रह्म)

द्‌+म=द्म (पद्म) द्‌+य=द्य (पद्य)

The following forms may also be noted :

श्‌+र = श्र (श्री)

Combined Forms of Consonants (संयुक्त व्यंजन)

k — ka	क्क,	क्क	पक्का, पक्का
k — kha	क्ख		मक्खी
k — ca	क्च		लेक्चर
k — ta	क्त		भक्त, भक्त
k — ma	क्म		रुक्मिणी
k — ya	क्य		वाक्य, क्या
k — ra	क्र		चक्र
k — la	क्ल, (क्ल)		क्लान्ति, क्लान्ति

k — va	क़, क्व	पक़, पक्व, क्वार
k — sa	क्स	अक्स

क्च Combination is met in words of English origin only.

Nasal and Nasalization

Anusvār, as the word indicates. comes after a vowel. Anu—after, svar—a vowel. Anusvār is a sign to represent any nasal letter (ङ् ञ् ण् न् म्) Anunāsik is a sign which represents nasalization of a vowel and it is pronounced with a vowel. A vowel may be an ananunāsik (अननुनासिक) or anunāsik (अनुनासिक) as अ or अँ. It is not correct to say that nasalization is a weaker form of anusvār. Thus while अं is अन् (an) अँ is nasalized अ, बं is ब्+अ+न् but बँ is ब्+अँ. The difference between the two should be carefully noted. We are giving below two words to illustrate the difference :

हंस-हँस, रंग-रँग

The first forms are nouns and the second forms are verbal roots.

A nasal combines only with the first four letters of its own class or with य, र, ल, व and श, ष, स, ह।

A nasal in Sanskṛt words is optionally replaced by anusvār in Hindī गङ्गा—गंगा, पुञ्ज—पुंज, कण्ठ—कंठ, मन्द—मंद, कम्प—कंप। But if a nasal is followed by another nasal or य it should not be replaced by anusvār. जन्म not जंम, कन्या not कंया, अम्मा not अंमा, मुन्ना not मुंना। If म् occurs at the end of a prefix and is followed by a consonant, it is changed into anusvār.

सम्+सार=संसार, सम्+देश=संदेश

The Chandravindu (ँ) is used in अ आ इ उ ऊ ए only (as in writing these vowels, any part of the letters is not above the upper line) as अँधेरा, आँख, इँदारा, उँगली, ऊँट, एँड़ी but in writing ई, ऐ, ओ, औ anusvār is often used, though phonetically Chandravindu would have been proper and desirable. Thus ऐंचा for ऐँचा, ओंठ for ओँठ, औंधा for औँधा are in use. Because the vowels इ, ई assume ि, ी as their mātrā forms, so when they are used with consonants, anusvār is generally written in such cases also, when Chandravindu would have been proper. Thus सिंचाई for सिँचाई, छींट for छीँट is written. Also vowels ए ऐ ओ औ with consonants are generally written with anusvār aud not Chandravindu as में for मेँ, मैं for मैँ, सोंठ for सोँठ and चकाचौंध for चकाचौँध ।

N. B. Hindī has a tendency towards nasalization. In many Sanskṛt words with anusvār, in course of change we find chandravindu in the tadbhava form दन्त—दाँत, मुण्ड—मूँड़ । In many Sanskṛt words even when there is no anusvār, the tadbhava forms have anunāsik.

मुच्छ—मूँछ, पुच्छ—पूँछ, निद्रा—नीँद

Anunāsik is seldom seen in Sanskṛt words, which are used in Hindī. It is met with in non-Sanskṛt words only.

When an anusvār is used, its pronunciation is approximately as follows :—

1. as ङ, before क, ख, ग, घ in Sanskṛt words शंका śankā, शंख śankha, तरंग taranga and जंघा janghā. In Hindī words, in common speech, anusvār is pronounced as न् as कंकड़ Kankaṛ, पंखा pankhā, नंगा nangā कंघा Kanghā.

2. as म् before प फ ब भ and व ।

कंपन Kampan, कंबल Kambal, खंभा Khambhā, संवत् Samvat.

3. as ञ् in संयम sanyam, संयुक्त Sanyukta.

4. as न् before त थ द ध; च छ ज झ, ट ठ ड ढ ।

Classification of letters on the basis of their pronunciation

Vowels	(स्वर)	Short ह्रस्व	Long दीर्घ
Guttural	(कंठ्य)	अ	आ
Palatal	(तालव्य)	इ	ई
Labial	(ओष्ठ्य)	उ	ऊ
Lingual or Cerebral.	(मूर्धन्य)	ऋ	

Diphthongs (संयुक्त स्वर)

Palatal	ए	ऐ
Labial	ओ	औ

Consonants:—	Surd (अघोष)	Surd asp (अघोष महाप्राण)	sonant (घोष)	sonant asp (घोष महाप्राण)	Nasal
Guttural	क	ख	ग	घ	ङ
Palatal	च	छ	ज	झ	ञ
Lingual	ट	ठ	ड	ढ	ण
Dental	त	थ	द	ध	न
Labial	प	फ	ब	भ	म

Semivowels (अन्तःस्थ)			Sibilants (ऊष्म)
Palatal	य		श
Lingual	र		ष
Dental	ल		स
Labial	व	Aspirate	ह

Pronunciation of Vowels

The Hindī vowels represent the sound of vowels in the following English words :

अ is approximately pronounced like u in *suggest* or *hut.*

आ is approximately pronounced like a in *father* or *far.*

इ is pronounced as ī in *fit* or *pin.*

ई is pronounced as ɪ in *deed* or *feet.*

उ is pronounced as u in *put* or *pull.*

ऊ is pronounced as oo in *fool* or *tool.*

N. B. When इ or उ comes after a consonant and as a final in a word, its pronunication is very short as in स्तुति or ऋतु. ऋ is pronounced as ri in *drink* or *bring*. Kellog rightly points out, "theoretically ऋ differs from रि in that the tongue-vibrating is not allowed to touch the gums as in consonant र. But this distinction is never regarded in practice."*

***Kellog** :—Hindi Grammar, p 13

ए is pronounced as e in *they.*

ऐ is pronounced as a in *mad* or *bad*

ओ is pronounced as o in *opaque* or *go.*

औ is pronounced as ou in *stout,* according to Greaves.

The pronunciation of ऐ and औ is to be carefully noted as they are pronounced differently in Sanskṛt and pure Hindī words. The pronunciation of these two vowels ऐ and औ are difficult for English-speaking people, as such pronunciation is not generally common in English words.

According to Greaves, it is difficult to pronounce ए ऐ ओ औ correctly. In Hindī words ऐ is often pronounced as a in 'an' and 'at'—a very short e, yet not a quite diphthong e.g. बैल, मौज. In Sanskṛt works ऐ is pronounced as if it is अइ ai and औ as if it is अउ and they are clear diphthongs.

As already mentioned, short ए and ओ are also found in a few words in Hindī as एक्का, एलावा, सेहरा, मेहतर, ओसारा, मोहल्ला. Because of this short pronunciation of ए and ओ sometimes optional forms with इ and उ are also used. एग्यारह, इग्यारह, मोहल्ला, मुहल्ला.

Pronunciation of inherent अ

It deserves special consideration. We have seen that there is an inherent अ in all the consonants. This inherent अ when it comes as a final (i.e. at the end of a word) is silent or unpronounced. Thus पागल Pāgala and पाप Pāpa are pronounced as पागल् and पाप् (Pāgal and Pāp) Within a word also, the inherent अ is silent at some places. It cannot be silent in the first letter of a word. This also is not silent, when it is preceded or followed by another silent अ.

Thus	सपना	is Sapnā	not Sapana
	कहता	is Kahtā	not Kahatā
	कटहल	is Kathal	not Katahal
	नगर	is Nagar	not Nagara

नगर is न्+अ+ग्+अ+र्+अ. In नगर, अ is at three places but the first अ cannot be silent as it is the first letter. The last अ must be silent as it is at the end of the last letter. Now the second letter cannot be silent. But in कटहल, क्+अ+ट्+अ+ह्+अ+ल+अ Katahala, the last अ must be silent, the first अ must not be silent. The third अ is not silent, because it is followed by a silent अ in ल at the end of a word. अ in the second letter is silent, because it is preceded by अ which is pronounced and followed by अ in ट which is also pronounced.

But the following exceptions to this general rule may be noted :

1. If न, त, र etc are used as words, e.g. र अन्तःस्थ अक्षर है।
2. If the final अ is in conjunct letter of a word, it is slightly pronounced, as सत्य Satya कर्म Karma and इन्द्र Indra.

N. B. This final अ is slightly or faintly pronounced. I do not agree with Shri Kāmta Prasād Guru who says that it is fully pronounced.[1]

In my opinion to pronounce fully final अ in धर्म is not correct. If अ is pronounced fully it will be the Sanskṛt mode of pronunciation, rather than that of Hindī. This inherent अ is pronounced faintly and according to Kellog might be represented by an apostrophe instead of a. Thus he prefers to write अन्नदाता *anndātā* rather *annadātā*. In pronouncing अन्न *anna*, the final अ is not fully pronounced.

3. If य comes after इ, ई, अ, as प्रिय *priya* इन्द्रिय *Ind iya.*
4. In poetry the final अ is sometimes pronounced. But in a large number of metres, the final अ in words coming at the end of a line, is not pronounced. When pause (यति) is on a word having a final अ it is not pronounced.

Pronunciation of Consonants

Gutturals

क — it is pronounced as k in *keep*.

ख — it is aspirated क

1. Hindi Vyakaran—P. 46

ग — it is pronounced as g in *goal.*
घ — it is aspirated ग

Palatals

ङ — it is pronounced as n in *king.*
च — it is pronounced as ch in *chain.*
छ — it is aspirated च
ज — it is pronounced as j in *jet,*
झ — it is aspirated ज
ञ — it is pronounced like the sharp sound of n in *punch.*

Cerebrals

ट — it is pronounced as t[1] in *take.*
ठ — it is aspirated ट
ड — it is pronounced as d[2] in *dog .*
ढ — it is aspirated ड
ण — it is pronounced like n with the tip of the tongue curled backwards and touching the hard palate. It has no equivalent in English.

Dentals

त — it is pronounced as t in Italian language. It is dental, and in all dental letters the tip of the tongue is spread out touching the upper teeth.

थ — it is aspirated त
द — it is pronounced as d in the Italian language.
ध — it is aspirated द
न — it is pronounced as n.

---

1. According to Kellog ट t and ड d have no precise equivalents in English. "In pronouncing them the tongue should be thrown well back, so as to strike, not the gums as in the English t and d, but the roof in mouth."—Kellog. p. 15.
2. The Englishman finds difficulty in pronouncing as the sound of त and द does not exist in the English language.

Labials

In pronouncing these letters the lips are pressed together and then separated.

प — it is pronounced as p in *pen.*
फ — it is aspirated प
ब — it is pronounced as b in *but.*
भ — it is aspirated b
म — it is pronounced like m.

N. B. In the above five classes, the first and third letters are called अल्पप्राण *alpaprāṇ* and the second and fourth महाप्राण *mahāprāṇ.* In pronouncing the 10 mahapran (aspirated) letters, a faint-sound of ह् is heard, mixed up with the previous alpaprāṇ letter. There is no visible sign of this mixing of ह् sound in the mahāprāṇ, but in representing it in the Roman script, the mixing or combination of the two sounds is indicated by the presence of h. The aspirate letter is pronounced by utteriug the smooth consonant with a forcible aspiration.[1]

ड़ and ढ़

These letters are written by placing a dot under ड and ढ "Great care should be taken to acquire the correct pronunciation of this letter, which is undoubtedly, for western organs, the most difficult of all the Hindī sounds, very few Europeans ever give it correctly." Kellog's direction is "to utter this correctly, place the tongue in the same position as for ड d and try to pronounce r, the proper sound will be given." (p. 15). They are also cerebral consonants and are called "retroflex flapped consonants." "They are pronounced by curling the lip of the tongue backwards and by

1. "Each of the above consonants has its aspirate ; i. e., it is combined with the spiritus asper so as to form but one vocal utterance. The same direction applies to the pronunciation of all the aspirates. viz. utter the smooth consonant with a forcible expiration ; the corresponding aspirates will then be given." Kellog. p. 16.

flapping i. e. strikiug with jerk, against as wide an area of the hard palate as possible." ढ is aspirated ड .

ड़ and ढ़ sounds have no place in Sanskṛt and are pure Hindī sounds. The effect of Hindī ड़ is so much that even Sanskṛt words like नाडी, पीडा, क्रीडा etc. are pronounced as नाड़ी, पीड़ा, क्रीड़ा and are often written as such.

Here we may note some peculiarities about the use of ड ḍ and ढ ḍh and ड़ ṙ and ढ़ ṙh.

1. While ड and ढ come as the first letter of a word ड़ and ढ़ do not.

2. ङ may be combined with ड and ढ but ड़ and ढ़ are not not combined with ड़ and ढ़ .

3. After an initial letter with anusvār ड or ढ follows, but after an initial letter with Chandravindu ड़ follows.

चंडी, मंडप, हंडा, गुंडा,
माँड़, मँड़वा, खाँड़ा

4. ड़ and ढ़ cannot come as initial letter ; however, they may come in the middle or end of a word.

सड़क, पकौड़ी, चढ़ाई, गढ़

These hints indirectly help in learning the pronunciation of ड़ and ढ़ ।

Semivowels

य — it is pronounced as y in *yet.*
र — it is a 'rolled' and voiced consonant.
ल — it is pronounced as l in *lake.*
व — it is pronounced as v in *very.* Its sound is intermediate between v and w.

श ष—it is pronounced like *sh* in shirt. In pronouncing श the tongue is thrown further forward and in pronouncing ष further back. According to Whitney, श is produced with the flat of the tongue against the forward part of the palatal arch and ष is produced with the tip of the tongue reverted into the dome of the palate. According to Greaves, some suggestions as to the difference may be found in the pronunciation of the two English words *sheet* and *shoot.* The difference in pronunciation of श and ष is not generally observed even by Indians.

स — It is a dental sibilant aud in pronouncing it the tongue touches the teeth instead of the gums.

ह — In pronunciation it is similar to 'h' in English. It is a 'voiced' and 'fricative' consonant.

: Visarga. "It has the sound of a voiceless ह fn Hindi." : h appears to be merely a sound. breathing a final *h*—sound (in the European sense of *h*) uttered in the articulating position of the preceding vowel—Whitney, p. 23. It is guttural and is pronounced by forcing *h* sound ont of the vocal organ with a slighter intensity. It generally comes in Sanskṛt words only as अन्तःकरण, दुःसह, प्रायः. In a few Hindī words also it is sometimes used, as छिः ।

क़ ख़ ग़ ज़ फ़

These few letters are used to write some foreign words in Hindī, when writers intend to retain their original pronunciation. ज़ and फ़ are similar to z and f in English. क़ is voiceless. It is produced by pronouncing क as far back in the throat as possible. ख़ and ग़ are fricative consonants.

ज्ञ—This conjunct letter—(ज्+ञ्=ज्ञ) is pronounced as gya (ग्+य्+अ) in Hindī. Some Sanskṛtists pronounce it as ज्+ञ् but this is not the common pronunciation in Hindī area.

Accent

Accent is less marked in Hindī than in English. Hindī has stress-accent but is not as distinctly audible, as for example in English. As its alphabet is phonetic, it presents little difficulty in pronunciation. But to a foreign reader, the accent in Hindi is not so easy, because, as we have said, it is not distinctly audible.

The following rules regarding accent, will serve as useful guide.

1. A letter coming before the last consonant with unpronounced inherent अ is accented.

घर ghár चमक camák

2. A letter coming before a conjunct letter is accented—पथ्य pathya सत्य Satya.

3. Exception—The rule is not followed in case of म्ह, न्ह and ल्ह as in तुम्हारा, उन्हें, सिन्हा, कुल्हाड़ी, आल्हा. In the opinion of some scholars म्ह, न्ह and ल्ह are to be treated as aspirated forms of म् न् and ल् and not as conjunct letters. But नन्हा is an exception, it is *nan-hā*.

4. A letter followed by visarga is accented—दुःख, अन्तःकरण.

5. The inherent अ in the initial letter is always slightly stressed—मन mán धन dhá-n.

6. A vowel coming before इ, उ and ऋ is slightly stressed.

इ—हरि Hari, कवि Kavi
उ—मधु Madhu, बहुत Bahut चतुर Catur
ऋ पितृ pitri

7. In verbs the accent is on the stem and not on the tense-marker.

		stem		tense-marker
करूँगा	—	करूँ (र्+ऊँ)		गा
कहता	—	कह	—	ता
चल	—	चल		आ (ा)
सुना	—	सुन	—	आ (ा)
आएगा	—	आ	—	ए+गा

8. In words having four letters and ending in unpronounced अ, the inherent अ in the second lettter is not accented ; the first two are pronounced together and the second two also together.

अनबन	as	अन्बन्	and not as	अन बन
सर पट	as	सर् पट्	and not as	सर पट
गड़बड़	as	गड़् बड़्	and not as	गड बड

Even where the four letters have different mātrās, there is a slight pause between the two parts in pronunciation.

मानसिक as मान्+सिक
पौराणिक as पौरा+णिक
उच्चारण as उच्चा+रण
तलवार as तल्+वार

9. In words formed by Sanskṛt prefixes (उपसर्ग) the prefix is distinctly pronounced.

उपवास as उप+वास
अनुरोध as अनु+रोध
प्रतिकार as प्रति+कार
प्रहार as प्र+हार
अमृत as अ+मृत

10. In words consisting of three letters and ending in a long vowel, the inherent अ in the second letter is not accented.

बकरा as बक्रा
हमला as हम्ला

11. In compound words the inherent अ in the last letter of the first part is not accented.

देवलोक is देव् लोक
सोमनाथ is सोम्नाथ

12. The first long vowel in a word is accented.

सोच Sŏc खेद Khèd

13. In a word consisting only of short mātrās the last but one is accented.

कठिन *Kathī'n* दिन *dī'n*

CHAPTER II

Words in Hindī

Hindī is rich in vocabulary as its words come from many stocks, both Aryan and non-Aryan. Hindī is a language of North India, known as Āryāvarta in ancient India, where Sanskṛt or Prākṛts and later Apabhranśa languages were spoken. Thus, it is natural that Sanskṛt should be the main source of a very large number of words in Hindī. Hindī is, linguistically speaking, a growth of that ancient speech of the land, whose elegant and cultured form was Sanskṛt and the vulgar or dialect form was Prakṛt in its various forms. The foreign words in Hindī, though they are also in thousands, came in the language mainly after 1000 A. D., when the Muslim invasions began to be felt in Hindī area and the Muslims began to settle here. Later, when the European powers came to this country in the 16th. century, some European words also entered into the language. The foreign pockets in those days were outside the proper Hindī area. After the establishment of British power in Hindī area, quite a large number of English words gained currency. The Persian and Arabic and the European words (mainly English), which entered in the language due to foreign domination and influence were mainly loan words consisting of nouns and a few adjectives. Thus an analysis of Hindī words would show that a large number of nouns and all pronouns, almost all verbs and adverbs and all prepositions, conjunctions and interjections are of Sanskṛt origin. The grammatical apparatus of the Hindī language is also greatly influenced by Sanskṛt. The non-Aryan languages of India, such as Dravidian aad Kolerian have given very few words to Hindī.

Hindī words may be classified into the following groups in accordance with their origin or derivation.

1. Tatsama (तत्सम) 'same as that'
2. Tadbhava (तद्भव) 'born of that'

3. Foreign (विदेशी)

4. Non-Aryan Indian Words (देशी)

Tatsama—Sanskṛt words when they are used in their original form are called Tatsama, such as जल, पवन, शरीर, मधुर, भोजन, आकाश, etc.

Tadbhava—Sanskṛt words, when they are used in a modified form, that is, after undergoing some changes in form.

रात	रात्रि,	दूध	दुग्ध,	हाथ	हस्त,
पहर	प्रहर,	नींद	निद्रा,	साँझ	सन्ध्या।

N.B.—Tatsama and Tadbhava words are generally used only with Sanskṛt words or words derived from Sanskṛt. But they may also be used for words of another language. If a word is used in the form in which it is in the language of origin, it is tatsama, but if it is used in a modified form, it is tadbhava. Thus लालटेन is tadbhava and लैन्टर्न is tatsama form of 'lantern', an English word. Similarly मे (May) is tatsama and मई tadbhava form of 'May', लाट is tadbhava and लार्ड is tatsama form of 'Lord.' This distinction may also be illustrated with reference to some Urdū words, e. g.

गरीब is tadbhava, ग़रीब is tatsama ; फायदा is tadbhava and फ़ायदा is tatsama.

Some Hindī grammarians also recognise a sub-class Ardha-tatsama between the Tatsama and Tadbhava. Ardha-tatsama words are such words which have come into Hindī directly from Sanskṛt and not through the stages of Prākṛt or Apabhranśa. Such words are nearer to Sanskṛt forms than their corresponding Prākṛt or Apabhranśa forms, if any.

Thus धरम and करम are nearer to धर्म and कर्म Sanskṛt than to धम्म and कम्म Prākṛt.

Sometimes the same Sanskṛt word has gives birth to several forms, one Ardha-tatsama and another tadbhava. Thus कारज and काज both are derived from कार्य, करम and काम from कर्म।

The foreign words in Hindī are either from the languages of Muslim countries of Asia or from some modern European languages. We may further subdivide them into two groups :

1. Arabic, Persian, Turkish etc.
2. English, Portuguese, French etc.

Of the foreign languages, Persian and English have given a large number of words. Arabic words have also come generally through Persian. Many of these foreign words have so much been a part of the common speech that they have to be treated for all practical purposes as Hindī words. They are like old settlers from another country, who have completely merged with the life of the country, adopted by them. Such words are कागज Arabic, कम Persian, चाकू Turkish, बटन and पेन्सिल English, कमरा and तौलिया Portuguese, अंग्रेज French, which are difficult to be replaced or avoided.

Non-Aryan Indian Words (so-called 'Deśī')

As regards the words borrowed or derived from the Dravidian or Kolerian languages we should remember that their number is very small. To call them only as Deśī is a misnomer. Sanskṛt words, either Tatsama or Tadbhava are also Deśī, belonging to this country (Deśī). Really speaking under this head are included all such words, whose derivation or origin is not definitely known.

Examples of such words are मूँगा 'खोट' पिल्ला etc.

The importance of this classification of words into Tatsama, Tadbhava and foreign classes will be apparent when several rules which govern words of particularly one class and not the other, will be given.

It has been said that 'no rules can be given for ascertaining the origin of a word' (Basic Grammar p. 24) But as this classification is of considerable importance, attempt should be made to formulate some rules for the guidance of the reader.

Note. Hindī, we have seen, is a natural linguistic growth or evolution of that ancient speech, which is known in its standard literary form as Sanskṛt and whose popular colloquial form may be termed as Prākṛt. In Hindī, Tadbhava words are said to be the corrupt forms of Sanskṛt or pure forms. Really speaking these Tadbhava words are our own and the Sanskṛt words constitute the linguistic heritage, which Hindī, in common with other modern Indian languages, has acquired by inheritance. This priceless treasure of Sanskṛt vocabulary has always gone to enrich the language and poets like Vidyāpati, Sūrdās and Tulsidās, all learned in Sanskṛt tradition, have profusely drawn words from that rich language. The Santa poets were more inclined to the use of Tadbhava forms, and it was natural for them as they were generally ignorant of Sanskṛt and came from the lower strata of society. Since the adoption of Khaṛī Bolī form of Hindī, a dialect of Western U. P., as the lingua franca of the country and since its patronage by the East India Company, Khaṛī Bolī became a literary speech. An early specimen of Khaṛī Bolī prose, Premsāgar, written under State patronage, showed a marked tendency towards Tatsama forms, The influence of Bengalī prose also encouraged the greater adoption of Sanskṛt words in Hindī prose and later Khaṛī Bolī poetry showed greater dependence on the Sanskṛt vocabulary to give its style a literary elegance and grandeur. This tendency grew and we find that the poetry of Chāyāvādī School (Romantic School, we may say) is more Sanskṛtised than in any period before. Thus in Hindī, it sometimes makes the style a little pedantic and artificial and Sanskṛt words are used, where Tadbhava forms could have served the purpose. To a non-Hindī reader, specially a foreigner, it becomes difficult to recognise a word, whether it is Tatsama or Tadbhava, because he finds them all intermingled.

An attempt is here made, perhaps for the first time, to give some rules for the guidance of readers.

All such native words are Tatsama generally,

1. in which the following letters occur श, ष, ङ, ञ, ण, or conjunct letters formed from these letters.

2. in which the following conjunct letters occur क्क, क्म, क्ल, क्त, ख्य, ग्ण, ग्ल, घ्र, च्य, ज्य, ज्ञ, ट्र, ठ्य, ड्र, त्र, त्व, त्क, त्न, त्य, त्स, द्म, द्य, द्र, द्व, ध्र, प्र, प्त, प्न, प्ल, ब्ज, ब्द, ब्ध, ब्र, भ्य, भ्र, म्र, म्ल, ल्म, ल्व, व्य, व्व, य्य, स्क, स्ख, स्म, स्र, ह्न, ह्य, ह्ल, ह्व

3. Conjunct letters formed by ऋ as कृ, शृ, पृ. नृ etc.

4. Words formed by the following Sanskṛt prefixes प्र, अन् (as अनादि, अनन्त etc) अनु, अप, अभि, उत् , उप दुर् , दुस् , निः निर् , परि, प्रति, वि, सम् ।

5. Words formed by अधः, अन्तर् , इति, कु, का पुनर् , पुरस् , प्राक् , बहिर् बहिस् , स्व, सह or स and used as prefixes.

6. Compound words in which the first part has a consonant or visarga at the end.

7. Words formed by adding Sanskṛt suffixes.

8. When the following occur at the end of a compound : कर (as दिवाकर, सुखकर), ग (as खग, नग), चर (as गोचर, वनचर), ज (as जलज, मनुज, अनुज), द (as सुखद, जलद), धर (as जलधर, भूधर), धि (as (जलधि, पयोधि), प (as नृप, मधुप), स्थ (as गृहस्थ, तटस्थ) ज्ञ (as सर्वज्ञ, कृतज्ञ, अज्ञ)

Words as Parts of Speech

A word is a letter or a combination of letters used to express an idea. आ means *come* and ऐ and ओ may be used as words as in ए लड़के, ओ लड़के, 'O boy !' As a consonant is followed by a vowel, a word may be monosyllabic as खा, जा, तू, को, से etc. Even a consonant with an inherent vowel may be a word as न (equivalent to 'no' in English). Thus a word in Hindī may be monosyllabic (एकाक्षरी) as जा, रो, दो etc or bisyllabic (द्वयक्षरी) रोना, देना or polysyllabic (अनेकाक्षरी) as एकता, भारत, चकमकाहट.

A word may be such, which changes its form (विकारी) or it may be such which does not (अविकारी). A word which does not change its form in gender, person or number is called Avyaya

(Indeclinable) by Hindī grammarians. Words like क्या, को, से etc are Avyaya. Therefore words are of two kinds (i) Vikārī (ii) Avikārī (Avyaya).

There are eight parts of speech : 1. Noun, 2. Pronoun, 3. Verb, 4. Adjective, 5. Adverb, 6. Preposition, 7. Conjunction and 8. Interjection. We may place the first four into one class and the rest into another.

Modern Hindī grammarians have also preferred to adopt this classification of parts of speech under the influence of English grammar[1]. However many scholars would like to have only six classes: 1. Noun, 2. Pronoun, 3. Adjective, 4. Verb, 5. Adverb and 6. Indeclinable (Avyaya). In my opinion this classification is better.

There is no difference in the concept of noun, pronoun or adjective in English or Hindī and therefore we will not go to define them. A noun is the name of a person or thing, which may be real or imaginary or a mere quality. Therefore the ancient grammarians preferred to call it नाम, though the word संज्ञा is in

---

1. Hindī grammar was neglected by Indian writers. It is strange that in the land of Pāṇini and Patañjali with a great tradition of Sanskṛt grammar and later also of Pāli, Prākṛt and Apabhranśa grammars, no attempt was made to write a systematic grammar of Brajbhāṣa or Avadhī, not to say of Kharī Bolī, which came into prominence in early 19th century. Foreign writers were pioneèrs in writing Hindī Grammar and Kellog's scholarly work still commands respect in the field. Before Guru Etherington's Bhāṣā Bhāskar was a popular book as it found a place in school syllabus. It was the treatment of the subject by these foreign writers that influenced many Hindī grammarians including Guru, for adopting the English method of writing grammar. Thus many grammatical terms and definitions were accepted or adopted on the pattern of English grammar.

greater use in Hindī grammars. A thing may be either Concrete (पदार्थवाचक) or Abstract (भाववाचक). The name may be of a particular being or thing or of a class, that is, it may be either Proper (व्यक्तिवाचक) as गंगा or Common (जातिवाचक) as नदी. We may consider a thing as an individual (व्यक्ति) or as belonging to a class (जाति). It is also classified as Collective (समुदाय वाचक) as भीड़ (crowd) and Material (द्रव्यवाचक) as तेल, घी. This classification as Collective and Material is not of much grammatical importance in Hindī. A भाववाचक (Abstract noun) denotes some quality (गुण), state (अवस्था) or action (व्यापार) only and not the thing possessing it.

CHAPTER III

Gender

The Hindī grammar recognises only two genders, masculine and feminine. It does not recognise neuter as is done in English, Sanskṛt and many other languages. A word denoting an inanimate object is either masculine or feminine. It is therefore difficult to know the gender of a word, which has to be learnt from usage or a good dictionary. Grammar may formulate certain rules for guidance, but sometimes they also are not very helpful. The terminations of a word are to be carefully observed, as many rules are based on these terminations. To understand the rules based on these terminations it is necessary to know the nature or origin of a word, whether it is Tatsama or Tadbhava or of foreign origin. We have given some rules to recognise a Tatsama word.

The gender of a word influences the form of the verb and also in many cases, the form of the adjective and the case-signs (Vibhaktis) following. The gender of a word denoting animate beings presents no difficulty, as the natural gender and grammatical gender is not different.

Gender of Tatsama words denoting inanimate objects

1. Tatsama nouns with inherent अ, are masculine, as ज्ञान धर्म, सत्य etc.

Exception—जय and words in which जय comes as the second part of the compound (as विजय, पराजय), देह, दाह, पुस्तक, शपथ etc. Also some words having य as the last letter as इन्द्रिय, विनय, सामर्थ्य, आय are feminine.

2. Tatsama nouns ending in आ are feminine, as माया, क्षमा आत्मा, दया etc.

Excep : देवता, तारा ।

Some writers use आत्मा as masc. because the Sanskṛt word is आत्मन् ।

3. Tatsama nouns ending in इ and ई are generally feminine. Exceptions : दधि, वारि, पाणि ।

N. B. The Hindus have endowed several physical or heavenly objects with life and on account of the influence of its mythology, full of symbolism. Planets. rivers, mountains etc. are also considered to be living objects and are masculine or feminine according to popular belief. Thus रवि (sun), शशि (moon), शुक्र (Venus), हिमालय, सागर, नदी, पृथिवी, आकाश, पवन are defined and their gender is determined by the belief whether they are देव or देवी (god or goddess). A river-name ending in आ or ई as गंगा, गोदावरी is fem. but ब्रह्मपुत्र, सिन्धु are नद and masc. A word may be masc. in one sense and fem. in another. Thus विधि (god of fate) is masc. but विधि (process) is fem. साक्षी a witness is masc. but साक्षी[1] (evidence) is fem.

Gender of Tadbhava Nouns

It is easier to know the gender of a Tadbhava noun, if one knows its Tatsama form, as its gender is generally the same as the gender of its corresponding Tatsama form, which may be ascertained with reference to the above-mentioned rules.

Some Tadbhava nouns with their corresponding forms are given below to illustrate it.

आंख (अक्षि), नाक (नासिका), भीख (भिक्षा), बांझ (बन्ध्या), सांझ (संध्या), दूब (दूर्वा), रात (रात्रि), जीभ (जिह्वा), घड़ी (घटा), मिट्टी (मृत्ती), पहर (प्रहर), अचरज (आश्चर्य), बादल (वारिद), मेह (मेघ), सुहाग (सौभाग्य), दूज (द्वितीया), अमावस (अमावस्या) ।

This may be given as a general rule, though there are some exceptions to it also. However the rule is helpful to those who can trace their Tatsama forms.

1. Tatsama ending in आ is fem. and Tadbhava ending in आ is masc.

---

1. मानो विनय की व्यग्रता की साक्षी दे रहा था । (Rangbhumi II p. 32)

2. Tatsama ending in अ is masc. and Tadbhava ending in अ is fem.

On analogy of Tadbhava words ending in आ, many other non-Sanskṛt words are also used as masc. as डेरा, झोला, जूता, गंडा etc.

There are a large number of words of non-Sanskṛt source, that is, neither they are Tatsama nor Tadbhava. It is rather difficult to know the gender of such words. The rule for making plural form of a word is important in this connection. If in making the nominative plural of a word, nasalization occurs, either as Chandravindu or Anusvāra. the word is feminine. Thus, because the plural form of चादर and इमारत are चादरें and इमारतें, they are feminine. But पत्ता and पेड़ are masc. because of their plural forms पत्ते and पेड़ । There is no nasalization here. This rule is a very valuable guide to know the gender of a word and is applicable to all kinds of words, either of Sanskṛt or non-Sanskṛt origin.

As regards English words, it is advisable to use them as masc. or fem. according to their form. If it ends in अ or आ it should be masculine and if it ends in ई it should be feminine. Thus सिनेमा चल रहा है। स्कूल खुला है। लाइब्रेरी खुली है। These are according to rules observed in case of Tadbhava words. But many writers give importance to the sense of the word and use accordingly. Thus कांग्रेस is feminine because it is a सभा (feminine) and मोटर is feminine because it is a गाड़ी . In such cases a word is used as masculine or feminine according to sense or sometimes on analogy of other similar words in common use.

Masculine terminations (पुंल्लिग प्रत्यय)

आ — (1) Verbs like पढ़ना, लिखना etc. used as verbal nouns.

(2)* Nouns ending in ना, having the form of a verb, as ढकना (ढक्कन) 'lid' and ओढ़ना a wrapper.

(3) Nouns formed by adding suffix आ to the stem as झगड़ा (झगड़+आ) घेरा (घेर+आ) जोड़ा (जोड़+आ)

---

* Rules for forming plural will be given while dealing with Number.

(4) Nouns signifying sound, formed by adding आका or आटा suffixes, as सन्नाटा (सन्न+आटा) भन्नाटा (घन्न+आटा) ई – When suffix ई signifies the possessor of some 'quality' as लोभी—(लोभ+ई) पापी (पाप्+ई) तेली (तेल+ई) or when it means belonging to or shows nationality as बंगाली (बंगाल+ई), मद्रासी (मद्रास+ई) ।

आव—Abstract nouns formed from verbal stems by adding suffix आव as बचाव (बच+आव) झुकाव (झुक+आप), फैलाव, बहाव etc.

आवा—Words formed by adding आवा to stems of casual verbs बुलावा (बुला+आवा), चढ़ावा (चढ़ा+आवा), दिलावा, बढ़ावा etc. एला, एरा—words formed by एला or एरा suffixes. अधेला=अध+एला, अँधेरा (अँध+एरा) ।

आक—Words formed by आक suffix.

तड़ाक=तड़+आक, धड़ाक=धड़+आक;

ड़ा—Words formed by ड़ा suffix.

मुखड़ा (मुख+ड़ा) टुकड़ा (टुक+ड़ा) दुखड़ा पन, पा—Abstract nouns formed by पन or पा suffixes.

पन—पागलपन, बचपन, छुटपन, बड़प्पन

पा—पुजापा (पूजा+पा) बुढ़ापा (बूढ़ा+पा), मोटापा रँड़ापा=रांड़+पा ।

आना—Words denoting country or place formed by आना suffix.

राजपूताना—राजपूत+आना (Country of Rajputs)

गोंडवाना—गोंड+आना (Country of Gonds)

आड़ी—Words formed by आड़ी suffix.

जुआड़ी=जुआ+आड़ी, खेलाड़ी=खेल+आड़ी,

आरी—Words formed by आरी suffix.

भिखारी=भीख+आरी, पुजारी=पूजा+आरी.

आर—Words formed by suffix आर meaning a place or a person.

भंडार=भंड+आर, कोठार=कोठ+आर,

चमार=चम+आर, लोहार=लोहा+आर, कुम्हार=कुम्भ+आर ।

इया— (1) Words formed by suffix इया meaning a worker.
धुनिया=धुन+इया, जड़िया=जड्+इया

(2) When meaning 'one who belongs to'. It also forms adjectives कन्नौजिया=कन्नोज+इया, कलकतिया=कलकत्ता+इया ।

(3) When meaning a cloth.

जांघिया=जांघ+इया, अंगिया=अंग+इया. मोटिया=मोट+इया ।

उवा—Words formed by उवा suffix meaning वाला or 'one who does'.

टहलुवा=टहल+उवा, पहरुआ=पहरा+उवा ।

ऊ—Words formed by ऊ suffix meaning 'one who does'.

खाऊ=खाऊ+ऊ, टट्टू=टट्ट+ऊ ।

जा —Words formed by suffix जा meaning 'a relation'.

भतीजा, भानजा, जीजा ।

एड़ी—Words formed by एड़ी meaning 'addicted to'.

गंजेड़ी=गांजा + एड़ी, भंगेड़ी=भांग+एड़ी

एरा—Words formed by एरा suffix.

बसेरा=बास बस+एरा, संपेरा=सांप+एरा, लुटेरा=लूट + एरा ।

वाल, वाला—Words by suffix वाल to place name—गाय वाल, प्रयाग वाल ।

वाला—मिठाई वाला, गाड़ी वाला

हार, हारा—Words formed by हार or हारा meaning 'one who carries some profession or occupation'.

चुड़िहार=चूड़ी+हार, लकड़ हारा ।

अक्कड़—Words formed by अक्कड़ suffix meaning 'doing something habitually'.

भुलक्कड़ 'forgetful' from भूलना 'to forget'

घुमक्कड़ 'wanderer' from घूमना 'to wander'.

ऐया—It is an agentive suffix.

गवैया=गा+ऐया—a singer.

Persian Suffixes

गर, गार—These Persian suffixes are added to Persian words to denote 'dealing in' as कारीगर artisan, सौदागर merchant, जादूगर magician, मददगार helper, गुनाहगार—Sinner.

दार—It denotes 'having'

जमीन्दार—Landlord. दूकानदार—Shopkeeper समझदार—One who understands easily.

बान—दरबान 'a doorkeeper'.

खोर—घुसखोर, चुगलखोर, हरामखोर।
खोर means 'one who eats'.

बाज—मुकदमाबाज, दगाबाज, धोखाबाज
बाज means 'addicted to'.

दान—कलमदान, पीकदान, उगलदान
दान—'a thing which contains'. Its feminine form is दानी—सुमादानी, धूपदानी।

चा —बागीचा—from बाग
चमचा—from चम
देगचा—from देग
Its feminine form is ची, बगीची, देगची,

आना—जुर्माना—जुर्म + आना
नजराना—नजर+आना
This आना is different from आना Hindi suffix meaning 'place'.

Feminine Terminations

ई — (1) When abstract nouns are formed by adding ई suffix to a root as बोली = बोल्+ई, हँसी = हस्+ई।

(2) Words formed by adding ई to an adjective as अमीरी (अमीर+ई)[1] गरीबी+गरीब+ई, खुशी = खुश+ई।

(3) Words formed by adding ई to indicate a profession महाजनी = महाजन्+ई, डाक्टरी = डाक्टर+ई, दलाली = दलाल्+ई।

(4) Words ending in ई as a diminutive suffix पोथी—from पोथा, रस्सी from रस्सा, डिब्बी from डिब्बा।

Many words ending in ई are feminine but at these places ई is not a suffix.
as सूई a needle, घड़ी a watch.

---

1. According to many grammarians अमीर+ई is अमीरी। But according to Sandhi rules अ+ई becomes ए and not ई, so in Hindi words for the purpose of Sandhi अमीर should be taken as अमीर् (because the inherent अ is not pronounced) and therefore अमीर्+ई=अमीरी. In adding Hindi suffixes and in Sandhi in non-Sanskṛt words, the inherent अ is not considered.

These words are Tadbhava forms of सूची and घटी in Sanskṛt and here ई is not a suffix.

Similarly पानी, जी, मोती, दही, घी, are not formed by suffix ई and are masculine because of their Tatsama forms पानीय, जीव, मौक्तिक, दधि, and घृत .

आई—(1) Words formed by adding suffix to adjectives meaning a quality as भलाई=भला+आई, बुराई=बुरा+आई, लम्बाई=लम्बा+आई.

(2) When added to a verbal stem meaning 'cost of labour or wages' as धुलाई (धुल+ आई), कमाई (कमा+आई), जुताई (जुता+आई) बुनाई (बुन+आई).

नी — Verbal stems having suffix as चटनी (चट+नी) कटनी, (कट+नी)

हट, वट — Verbal stems having हट or वट as suffix बुलाहट चिकनाहट, घबराहट, or दिखावट, सजावट etc.

ती — Verbal stems with ती suffix denoting abstract quality बढ़ती, घटती, भरती, गिनती etc.

आस — Verbal stems with आस :

प्यास=पी+आस, मिठास=मीठा+आस, खटास=खटा+आस

इया — It is a diminutive suffix :

लुटिया=लोटा+इया, फुड़िया=फोडा+इया, एरी, एली— Words formed by suffix एली :

as हथेली—हाथ+एल, रखेली=रख+एली, सहेली=सह+एली

की — Words formed by suffix की :

बैठकी=(बैठ+की), डुबकी= (डुब+की), फिरकी=(फिर+की)

त — Abstract nouns formed by suffix त — as रंगत, हजामत ।

री, ली — Diminutives formed by री or ली suffix :

छतरी=छाता+री, गठरी गाठ+री, टिकली=टीका+ली, बिंदली=बिंद+ली

Verbal stems ending in अ and used as nouns such as लूट, दौड़, प्रकार, चमक etc.

Abstract nouns formed by adding न to a verbal stem. रहन (रह verbal stem) जलन (जल a verbal stem)

List of common words which are masculine

(क) कुँआ, कीचड़, कंकड़, कछर, कड़ा, कद, कदम, कपड़ा, कफन, कब्ज़, कानू, काबू, किनारा, केसर, कोयल, कोठा, कीर ।

(ख) खँडहर, खंभा, खजाना, ख्याल, खिलाना, खमीर, खद्दर, खाता, खैर, खेवा, खुर, खीरा, खपड़ा ।

(ग) गट्ठर, गल्ला, गन्ना, गुलाब, गजब, गजरा, गला, गाँजा, घी, घंटा, घराना ।

(घ) घाव, घाम, घूँट, घूँघट, घोंसला ।

(च) चींचपड़, चश्मा, चालचलन, चकमा चक्कर, चम्मच, चलन, चाकू, चिराग, चुटकुला ।

(छ) छछूंदर, छाता, छिलका, छोट, छोह, छेद, छप्पर ।

(ज) जी, जाड़ा, जमघट, जोरा, जो, जवाब, जिगर, जाला ।

(झ) झींगुर, झंखाड़, झंडा, झगड़ा, झूठ, झूलन, झाड़ू ।

(ट) टीका, टुकड़ा, टोटका, टील ।

(ठ) ठट, ठट्ठा, ठप्पा, ठर्रा, ठाट-बाट, ठूँठ, ठेला, ढाँचा ।

(ड) डंक, डमरू, डील, डेरा, डोरा, डोलडाल ।

(ढ) ढक्कन, ढब, ढाँचा, ढोंग, ढाढ़स ।

(त) ताबीज, तौलिया, तकिया, ताश, तीतर, तारा, तकाजा, तेलहन, तीखुर, तीतर, तूलिया, तोड़ा, तोला, त्योहार ।

(थ) थान, थोक, थपेड़ा, थप्पड़ ।

(द) दही, दाँत, दस्तख़त, दंगल, दखल, दतुअन, दरगाह, दर्द, दरिया, दाद, दरिया, दाद, दस्तक, दहेज, दावात, दिमाग, दिलासा, दुखड़ा, दोपहर, दुपट्टा, दुश्मन ।

(ध) धुँआ, धनिया, धक्का, धड़का, धड़, धतूरा, धावा ।

(न) निचोड़, नीबू, नसीब, नक्शा, नखरा, नगीना, नशा, न्योता ।

(प) पद्य, पौधा, पिसान, पहिया, पैदावार, पनघट, पपीहा, परदा, परवल, पीपल, पैसा, प्यार, पहरा ।

(फ) फंदा, फक्कड़, फरमा, फरेब, फर्श, फौवारा ।

(ब) बाग, बगीचा, बोल बहाव, बंदनवार, बदला, बयान, बरछा, बलगम, बस्ता, बाँध, बादल, बादाम, बाल ।

(भ) भेड़िया, भंडार, भँवर, भरोसा, भात, भादो, भूलभुलैया, भोंपा ।

(म) मोती, मजा, मोजा, मतलब, मंडवा, मकोड़ा, मंशा, मंसूबा, मक्खन ।

(र) रिवाज, रुमाल, रफू, रव, रवा, रहम, रान, रास्ता, रूख, रोजगार, रोब, रोजा, रोड़ा ।

(ल) लेनदेन, लगान, लालच ।

(श) शरबत, शहद, शहतूत ।

(स) सूत, सफर, सौगात, संग, संतरा, सखुआ, सट्टा, सबेरा, सहारा, साफा, साथ, सामान, सुन्ना ।

(ह) हार, माला, हँड़िया, हथफेर, हथौड़ा, हमला, हवाला, हल्ला, हाट ।

List of common words which are feminine

Words ending in न

जलन, सड़न, सूजन, मरन, धुन, जान, बीन, लगन, शरन, उठान, अचकन, अनबन, उलझन, कतरन, पलटन, पहचान, फटकन ।

Words ending in क

कूक, चूक, फूँक, धाक, अटक, खटक, चटक, झिझक, झलक, तड़क, भड़क, पलक, महक, ठंडक, धमक, भनक. सड़क, बहक, धमक, सनक, झनक, ललक, लहक, चटक, मटक ।

Words ending in स, श

प्यास, आस, नस, बहस, रास, रिस, शिफारिश, ओस, घास, निकास, लाश, नालिस, उड़िस, साँस, कांग्रेस, पुलिस, कोशिश ।

Words ending in ह

चाह, राह, छाँह, आह, थाह, डाह, सुह, सुबह, जगह, वजह, परवाह ।

Words ending in र

पुकार, लकीर, नजर, दीवार, टक्कर, ठोकर, डगर, तलवार, धरोहर, पतवार, सरकार, भरमार, फुहार, बहम, बौछार, कचनार, चीत्कार, कछार, मीनार, हार, पराजय, ललकार, तकरार, अरहर, बटेर, तस्वीर, तहरीर ।

Words ending in ड़

जड़, आड़, अकड़, पकड़, रगड़, दौड़, मरोड़ ।

and खाल, खाट, खीझ, गच, घूस, चकाचौंध, भूल, चोंच, छाछ, छींट, छूट, जाँच, जायदाद, जेब, टाँग, टेर, टेव, टेंट, डाल, डाँट, ढाल, तड़प, तरफ, धूल, धूप, नकेल, नकल, पायल, डीठ, पीठ, पीब, बैठक, बर्फ, बगल, बाढ ,माँग, मदद, मंजिल, याद, रग, रास, राय, रीझ, खीझ, रीढ़, रेख, लगाम, लाज, लाग, लू, लोथ, शर्म, शाम, शकल, सँभाल, सूझ, हद, छींक, तार, मुसकान, चील, रेणु, ऋतु, धातु, साँझ, चितवन, बालू, मूँग, समझ, लूट, मेहराब, मिसाल, मशाल, दीमक, कोयल, मैना, श्यामा, मुनिया, चिड़िया, तूती, जोंक, कचबचिया, गौरैया, बुलबुल, लोमड़ी, सामर्थ्य, आँच, लहर, लौ, मूँछ, हवा, सजा, बला, दुआ, दफा, तमन्ना, दुनिया, मसूर, दाख, गाजर, दौलत, नौबत, रसीद, तरकीब, तमीज, पीतल, काँख, शराब, जूँ, छत, सरसों ।

CHAPTER IV

Number

Hindī also has two numbers only — Singular and Plural. Many Hindī words have the same form in plural. All masculine nouns except those ending in आ undergo no change in the plural. Thus भवन, ऋषि, पक्षी, साधु, भाई, डाकू, चौबे, रासो are not changed in plural. Therefore in these cases, plurality is denoted either by the context or by the form of the verb. Often plurality is denoted by the use of a numeral as चार विद्यार्थी, तीन साधु, दो डाकू or by an adjective of quality. In English plural sign s or es is invariably used to denote plurality, but in Hindī often the plural form is not used and plurality is denoted by the use of a numerical or the form of the verb only. Use of plural sign in case of feminine nouns is necessary. However, sometimes the plural form is not used in feminine nouns though it is grammatically necessary.

Plural Forms of Masculine Nouns ending in आ

1. आ is changed to ए as घोड़ा — घोड़े (घोड़्+ए) पंखा — पंखे (पंख्+ए)

Exceptions (1) काका, आजा, मामा, लाला, बाबा, नाना—All these words denote elderly relations and formed by repetition of the same letter.

But साला, भतीजा, भानजा, पोता, बेटा have their plural forms as साले, भतीजे, भानजे, पोते, बेटे. They are 'younger' relations.

(2) मुखिया and अगुआ

(3) Sanskṛt words like पिता, जामाता, देवता, युवा, योधा, etc. are also used in plural.[1]

---

1. Such words in Sanskṛt end in ऋ or न्. Their Noun Sing. forms are used in Hindī.

Plural Forms of Feminine Nouns

1. Words ending in अ —अ is changed to एँ; बात-बातें गाय-गायें
   ,, ,, ,, आ—यें is simply added; लता-लतायें विधवा-विधवायें
   ,, ,, ,, इ —याँ is simply added; रीति-रीतियाँ
   ,, ,, ,, ई —याँ is added after ई is changed to इ; रानी रानि-यां, टोपी-टोपि-यां ।
   ,, ,, ,, उ —यें is simply added.
   ,, ,, ,, ऊ—यें is added after ऊ is changed to उ; वघू-वधुयें
   ,, ,, ,, ओ—यें is simply added ; गौ-गायें

Words ending in या as चिड़िया, गुड़िया, बुढ़िया—sometimes आं (=) only is added—चिड़ियाँ, गुड़ियाँ, बुढ़ियाँ । Optional forms like चिड़ियायें, बुढ़ियायें are also used.

A Material or a Collective noun is used generally is singular. Thus सोना, दूध, पानी are used in singular. सामग्री, feminine collective noun, is often used in plural as सामग्रियां. In my opinion this use is undesirable. Where different varieties of a Material noun is intended, plural may be used.

Because of the influence of Persian and Arabic grammars on Urdū many plural forms governed according to rules of those languages, have crept in Hindī, through Urdū, which was a Court language for a very long period. Thus we have the following forms also :

साहेब	—	साहेबान,	मालिक	—	मालिकान
तारीख	—	तवारीख,	पटवारी	—	पटवारियान
ख्याल	—	ख्यालात,	कागज़	—	कागज़ात

N. B. In Hindī, rules of plural number are often not observed In writing, often in poetry and sometimes in prose also, writers have used singular forms, when plural forms would have been grammatically more appropriate. In common speech we often hear such expressions :

(1) दो रुपये की मिठाई लाओ (Bring sweets worth two rupees.)

(2) दो लात जमा दूँगा, बस ठीक हो जाओगे ।

(I will give you two kicks and you will be alright). Grammatically दो लातें would be correct.

Singular Words used as Plural

प्राण, भाग्य and दर्शन according to some grammarians should always be used in plural. But their singular use is also met in writings of good writers.

प्राण—न जाने कब प्राण निकलेंगे ? प्राण जाय तो जाय, झूठ नहीं बोलूँगा।

भाग्य—तुम्हारे भाग्य बड़े अच्छे हैं। मेरा ऐसा भाग्य कहां ?

दर्शन—आपके दर्शन वदे थे। (Premchand, Rangbhūmi p. 88) In my opinion it is unnecessary to insist upon their use in plural only. Grammar should follow usage.[1]

Some words having collective sense are used to denote plurality

लोग—जो लोग आ रहे हैं। बहुत लोग ऐसा कहते हैं।

लोग is Tadbhava from लोक. In modern Hindi लोग is used with pronouns as हम, तुम, वे. With nouns its use is not considered elegant. For धोबी लोग, कुली लोग, मजदूर लोग, धोबियों, कुलियों, मजदूरों are preferred. लोक should not be used with animals, as बन्दर लोग बकरी लोग।

गण—पाठक गण. Though गण (a class or a group) has collective sense it is used in the sense of readers. Similarly उडु गण for *stars.*

वृन्द—बालक वृन्द for "*Boys*".

जन in—गुरुजन, हरिजन। गुरुजन—*elders.* हरिजन—is used both as singular or plural.

Some words denoting collection of number

जोड़ा—pair, एक जोड़ा जूता, a pair of shoes.

जोड़ी—pair, बैलों की जोड़ी, a pair of bullocks or any cattle.

गाही—a collection of five (generally used in sellIng fruits etc).

कोड़ी—a collection of twenty (generally used by washermen).

---

1. प्रयोगशरणा हि वैयाकरणाः

बीसी—a collection of twenty.

गंडा—a collection of four (generally in use in fruit market etc.)

दर्जन—*a dozen*, corrupted from dozen.

N. B. —With the growing use of Sanskṛt words in literary Hindī in modern times, the use of Sanskṛt numerals is also increasing. But this tendency is not a healthy sign, for it is creating a gulf between the language of pandits and scholars and the language of the people. Sanskṛt ordinals upto eighteen are also largely used these days, so they are given below.

प्रथम, द्वितीय, तृतीय, चतुर्थ, पंचम, षष्ठ, सप्तम, अष्टम, नवम, दशम, एकादश, द्वादश, त्रयोदश, चतुर्दश, पंचदश, षोडश, सप्तदश, अष्टादश ।

Tithis

Of the Sanskṛt Tithis, the following are generally used, as they are auspicious and sacred on account of their association with religious rites and functions: अष्टमी (जन्माष्टमी), नवमी (रामनवमी), एकादशी, चतुर्दशी (अनन्त) and पूर्णिमा ।

In religious context, their Hindī equivalents are less popular.

Adjective Formation from Numerals

अकेला, *alone,* is formed by अक+एला where अक is a modified form of एक ।

दुकेला, *two persons only,* is formed by दु+केला

Like other adjectives ending in आ, अकेला, दुकेला are modified by gender and number—अकेला, अकेली, दुकेला, दुकेली ।

Similarly अधेला which is a noun and is a half-pice coin, अधेला= अध+एला ।

अधेली is fem. of अधेला; अधेली also means a half-pice coin, (in some areas it means half-rupee piece also). अधेला or अधेली coin is not issued now.

CHAPTER V

Person (पुरुष)

There are three parties to a speech — the speaker, the person spoken to and the person or thing spoken about. The speaker is the First Person (उत्तम पुरुष), the person spoken to is the Second Person (मध्यम पुरुष) and the person or thing about which some thing is spoken is the Third Person (अन्य पुरुष).

The subject of Person will be treated with the subject of Personal Pronouns. The three Persons are also grouped under two heads, Singular and Plural.

	S.	P.
1st Per.	मैं I.	हम We
2nd. Per.	तू Thou	तुम You
3rd. Per.	वह He, She, It.	वे They

CHAPTER VI

Case and Case–Signs कारक और कारक-विभक्ति

According to Sanskṛt grammarians, a case indicates the relation-ship of a word with the verb in a sentence and so they do not recognise Possessive (सम्बन्ध) or Vocative (सम्बोधन) as case. However, in Hindī, Guru defines case to be the form of noun or pronoun, by which its relationship with any other word in the sentence is indicated (Hindī Vyākaraṇ p. 274) and has, for various reasons, followed the English Grammar, by recognising them also as cases, besides Nominative (Kartā), Accusative (Karma), Instrumental (Karaṇ), Dative (Sampradān), Ablative (Apādān) and Locative (Adhikaran). For beginners, desirous of learning Hindī Grammar, through the English medium, the recognition of the Possessive or Genitive (सम्बन्ध) case and also the Vocative (सम्बोधन) may be helpful.

Case-Signs in Hindī.

The Sanskṛt Grammar has a special scheme of 21 case-endings (Sup सुप terminations), grouped into seven classes. In Hindī however, case-signs are few in number. They are used as post-positions though they serve the purpose of prepositions in English. Generally speaking **ने** is an exclusive case-sign of the Nominative. **को** is a case-sign of the Accusative but sometimes comes after the Dative and Locative also. **से** is case-sign of the Instrumental and Ablative. **के लिये** is the case-sign of the Dative. **में** and **पर** are the case-signs of the Locative case. In Hindī **को** and **से** are such case-signs which come in more than one case. In Hindī therefore few case-signs have fixed meaning or purpose and the same case-sign may have. different meanings at different places. For example, **को** (generally tbe case-sign of the Accusative) may also come for the Nominative In **राम को अभी खाना है** *'Ram has yet to eat'*, **को** comes after **राम** which is the subject in the sentence. In **लड़का खाने को गया है** *'The boy has gone to eat'*, it has the sense of 'for'. **से** is both Instrumental and Ablative case-sign.

Some writers are of opinion that the case-signs are a form of extreme suffixes (चरम प्रत्यय), as after a case-sign no other suffix can be added. However two case-signs may come together as में से, में का. It is proper to consider a case-sign as an Indeclinable (अव्यय) of a special kind. Except का sign of the possessive, other case-signs like ने, को, से, .में and पर are all Indeclinables. का has two other forms की and के and is not therefore an Avyaya. We have already said that according to Sanskṛt grammarians it is not a case (कारक).

A case-sign should be separately written except when it comes after a pronoun.

राम ने मुझे बुलाया था। गोपाल से मैं बातें करना चाहता था।

उसने मुझे बुलाया था। तुमसे मैं बातें करना चाहता था।

Before a case-sign, a noun comes either in its unmodified (Direct form) or in a slightly modified (Oblique) form.

Singular Oblique form :

In masc. nouns ending in आ

आ is changed to ए

बेटा=बेट्+आ, बेट्+ए=बेटे। बेटे ने, को, से, में, पर

There is no change in other words.

Plural Oblique forms : ओं is the sign of the oblique which is called Vikaraṇ by Hindī grammarians.

Before this ओं is added, final इ becomes इय्, final ई is shortened to इ final. उ undergoes no change final, ऊ is shortened to उ.

Masc. मुनि—मुन्+इय्+ओं—मुनियों

Fem. रीति—रीत्+इय्+ओं—रीतियों

Masc. हाथी—हाथ्+इय्+ओं—हाथियों

Fem. नदी—नद्+इय्+ओं—नदियों

Masc. साधु—साध्+उ+ओं—साधुओं

Fem. ऋतु—ऋत्+उ+ओं—ऋतुओं

Masc. भालू—भालु+ओं—भालुओं

Fem. बहू—बहु+ओं—बहुओं

At one time in the first decade of this century, a strong controversy had risen among scholars, whether a Vibhakti should be attached to a word or remain detached, that is, whether घर में or घरमें, रामसे or राम से is the proper mode of writing. But, now majority is in favour of writing case-signs separately. Hindi, though a successor language of Sanskṛt or Prākṛt, in course of its growth or development became an analytical language, so a case-sign should be written separately.

In nouns ending in ए, and औ simply ओं is added. चौबे—चौबेओं, जौ—जौओं.

In words ending in ओं, भादों—भादों. ओं in not added as it is already there, सरसों—सरसों. Here ओं is not added as it is already there भौं—भौंओं.

N. B. Words ending in ए, ओ, औ, ओ, औं are very few in Hindi.

N. B. Before a case-sign comes after a place-name ending in आ as दरभंगा, पटना etc आ is changed to ए. दरभंगे से, पटने में, कलकत्ते में and not दरभंगा से, पटना में, कलकत्ता में.

But this rule is observed only in case of place-names in India and not that of outside India. Even in India, often this rule is not observed in case of place-names ending in या, वा and आ as गया, रीवा, नाभा.

But अफ्रिका से, अमेरिका में. and not अफ्रिके से, अमेरिके में are correct.

In my humble opinion this rule should not be strictly observed and place-names being proper nouns should not be modified, when case-signs come after them.

Case-Signs (विभक्ति)

The Vibhaktis express various forms of relationship, which exist between a Noun (or Pronoun) and other words in a sentence such as subject, object, means, purpose, advantage, separation, origin, possession, material, composition, place, time etc. To express all these forms of relation only few case-signs (ने, को, से, का, की, के, में, पर) are used and so the appropriate use of these is very important. Its importance may be compared to the importance of the appropriate use of Prepositions in English Grammar. Of these six case-signs को and से are more important as they express different relations and while others ने and का (की, के) and में पर are generally used only as Nominative, Possessive and Locative case-signs.

(1) The unmodified (Direct form) Noun i. e. a Noun without case-sign, may be used either as a subject or object. Thus at many places, we see a Nominative without its case-sign (ने) or an object without its case-sign को.

मोहन पढ़ता है। पत्ते गिरते हैं। लड़की सोती है। स्त्रियां गा रही हैं। मैं खाऊंगा। वे कब आवेंगे।

In all these sentences, the nominative case-sign ने is not used with the subject of the sentence. The use of ने is restricted and when it is used the subject ending in आ takes the oblique form. लड़का—लड़के ने

(2) An object (कर्म) also often comes without its case-sign को—

मोहन रोटी खाता है। बढ़ई लकड़ी चीरता है। सीता खाना पकाती है। वह शरबत पीता है।

At these places we see that रोटी, लकड़ी, खाना and शरबत, all objects, come without their case-sign को. (Basic Grammar : p. 27.)

ने—It is exclusively used with the subject of a transitive verb in its past participle form. The subject is in its oblique form and the verb agrees with the object in number and gender.

ने does not come after the subject of the following transitive verbs. बकना, बोलना, भूलना, लड़ना, लाना and समझना (according to some writers).

The general rule is that past participle is formed by adding आ or य्+आ to the verbal root and ई (or य्+ई) to form its fem. form.

पढ़्—पढ़्+आ=पढ़ा	masc.	पढ़्+ई=पढ़ी	fem.
कह्—कह्+आ=कहा	,,	कह्+ई=कही	fem.
खा—खा–य्+आ=खाया	,,	खा+य्+ई=खायी (खाई)	fem.

etc.

राम ने फल खाया। राम ने फल खाये।
राम ने रोटी खायी। राम ने रोटियां खायीं।
लड़कों ने आम खाया। लड़कों ने आम खाये।
लड़कों ने किताब पढ़ी। लड़कों ने किताबें पढ़ीं।

(Mark that the form of the verb agrees with the number and gender of the object).

The proper use of ने may only be fully understood when the subject of tense and mood is treated.

N. B. According to philologists the expressions like राम ने and मोहन ने are derived from Sanskṛt Instrumental रामेण and मोहनेन. This ने is only found in some Western Ḥindi dialects.

को

It is generally used with the object of a transitive Verb and gives a certain definiteness to it. Therefore it is said to be an Accusative case termination. But it may also come after the subject in a sentence.

(*I have to eat*) मुझको खाना है।

(*Bharat has to read*) भरत को पढ़ना है।

It is also used in the Locative case e. g.

मैं शाम को आऊंगा। *I shall come in the evening.*

शाम को सभा होगी। *A meeting will be held in the evening.*

It is difficult to give rules as to where the use of को is necessary and where not. At several places, where it is used, it may be omitted at the option of the speaker or writer. Thus मैं बाजार को जाता हूँ and मैं बाजार जाता हूँ are both correct, but the latter is perhaps better. मैं घर जाता हूँ is better than मैं घर को जाता हूँ.

At such places को is superfluous. को is not necessary unless the speaker or writer intends to give an idea of definite-ness. to the place. When को comes for 'at' or 'in', it is not good and right to omit it. सांझ को मैं आऊँगा and not सांझ मैं आऊँगा, मैं दिन को चलूंगा और रात को तुम्हें आना होगा—at such places omission of को is not desirable. Sometimes omission of को may lead to confusion.

But in common speech we ask रात कहाँ थे ?

Where (you) were at night ? It should have been रात को or रात में तुम कहाँ थे ?

Generally को is omitted, if the object is a non-human-being or an inanimate object. राम ने घोड़ा खरीदा है। (not घोड़े को) गाड़ी खुलने दो (not गाड़ी को) मैं सिनेमा देखूँगा (not सिनेमा को).

को is generally used with बुलाना, पुकारना, कोसना, सुलाना, जगाना, बनाना.

उस लड़के को बुलाओ, पुकारो, जगाओ।

अब भाग्य को कोसने से क्या लाभ ?

मैंने भगवानप्रसाद को शिक्षक बनाया है।

को is used when the object is a Pronoun denoting a human-being. मैं तुमको खोजता हूं। वह किसको देखता है ?

N. B. The optional forms तुम्हें and किसे may also be used

When a Verb is in benedictive form, को is used. घोड़े को घास खिलाओ। प्यासे को पानी पिलाओ।

When there are two objects, को is used with the main object (मुख्य कर्म) and not with the secondary object. (गौण कर्म)

Greaves is of opinion that where there are two Accusatives, one of the so-called Accusatives is more strictly a Dative. But this view is not accepted by Hindi Grammarians. He gives an illustration.

The horse kicked the boy घोड़े ने लड़के को लात मारी। "According to Hindī grammarians it is the kick that the horse strikes, not the boy. 'The boy is the recipient of the kick and therefore in the Dative". In such a sentence the Hindī Grammarians recognise two objects, one लड़का and the other लात. The case-termination, is used with लड़का and not with लात. In my opinion the following rule is helpful in determining with which object the Accusative case termination को should be used.

1. If the speaker puts a question with क्या ? (what), the object of the Verb should be without को. क्या मारी ? लात ।

2. If the speaker puts a question with किसको ?, the object of the verb is used with को ।

किसको ? लड़के को ।

When Causative verbs like खिलाना, पिलाना etc. with two objects, are used, को is not used with the thing object but with the person object—

वह राम को रोटी खिलाता है ।

Here राम and रोटी both are objects, but को comes after the 'person object' राम and not the 'thing object' रोटी.

When there are more than one object, one complementing the other, को is used with the last object and the other objects preceding take the nominative form.

राम अपने भाई, तीन बेटे और बेटियों को लेकर प्रदर्शनी गया था ।

Here को comes after the last object बेटियों and not after भाई and बेटे. In this sentence note that there are three objects, (भाई, बेटे, बेटियों) but they are of the same kind, one complementing the other.

को Used For Dative सम्प्रदान

को when used in a Dative sense serves the purpose of के लिये (के निमित्त, के वास्ते, के अर्थ)

को is also a case-termination of the Dative. Generally, Grammarians regard के लिये and the case-sign of the Dative in Hindi but के लिये should not be treated as such. If के लिये is treated as a Dative case-sign, why not के निमित्त or के वास्ते or के अर्थ also. In fact लिये is a form of the root ले and has the sense of having taken. The case-sign should be one word and not two words.

When को comes after a Verb, the ending आ of the Verb is changed to ए—देखना, देखने (को)

१—वह मेला देखने को गया है ।

२—वह मेला देखने गया है।

३—वह मेला देखने के लिए गया है ।

All the above three sentences carry the same sense. In the second sentence को is omitted. In the third sentence के लिये has been used instead of को; को in the first sentence has Dative sense.

के लिये has the sense 'for' or 'for the purpose of'. In the following sentences को should not be omitted :—

खाने को कुछ नहीं मिलता। पहनने को कपड़ा कहां है? कहने को तो बहुत है। पढ़ने को एक किताब दो। रखने को रख दो यहाँ, पर मेरी जिम्मेदारी नहीं रहेगी।

Therefore when को comes after a Verb in a Dative sense and in the beginning of a sentence, its use is necessary.

But मैं खाने जाता हूँ may be used for मैं खाने को जाता हूं or मैं खाने के लिए जाता हूँ.

को is generally used with an Accusative of place and time, but often, even in such sentences को is omitted.

एक ओर को ले गया; एक ओर ले गया.

आज रात को तू यहीं ठहर जा; आज रात तू यहीं ठहर जा.

सब अपने अपने घर (को) चले गये.

At such places, really speaking, को has a locative sense and should be translated by 'at' in English.

आज रात को तू यहीं ठहर जा

'Stay here at night to-day.'

In speech, को is often omitted, and its omission is considered quite idiomatic.

It is very difficult to give any definite rule regarding the use of को. However the following illustrations will serve as a guide to those who learn Hindī as a foreign language.

१. खाने को जी नहीं चाहता।

२. मुझको अब मेल की उम्मीद नहीं।

३. तुमको मिठाई अच्छी लगती है।

४. मुझको अभी बहुत पढ़ना है।

५. क्या तुमने राम को मेरी कलम दी है?

६. शाम को चौक में बड़ी भीड़ रहती है।

७. किसी को बुला लाओ।

८. तुमको ऐसा न कहना चाहिए।

९. राम को इस समय जगाना ठीक नहीं।

१०. भिखमंगे को भीख दे दो।

११. गुरु को कठोर भी होना पड़ता है।

१२. विद्या को सम्मान मिलना ही चाहिये।

१३. कहने सुनने को बहुत है पर बात बढ़ाने से क्या?

१४. मरने को सभी मरते हैं, पर मरना उसी का मरना है, जिसे लोग मरने पर भी याद करें।

१५. कुल और जाति को महत्त्व देना इस युग में ठीक नहीं।

१६. राम अपनी स्त्री, भाई और बहनों को साथ लेकर सिनेमा गया था।

१७. लोगों को उनसे बड़ी मदद मिलती थी।

१८. हम लोगों को ऐसा लगता है कि महँगी अब नहीं जायेगी।

१९. हम लोगों को साग-सत्तू भी नसीब नहीं।

२०. बच्चों को भूत से बड़ा डर लगता है।

२१. तुमको साथ लेकर मैं बाजार जाऊँगा।

२२. बच्चों को लेकर कहीं सफर करना मुश्किल है।

२३. सबको घर के अन्दर बुलाना ठीक नहीं।

२४. जो दुःख को सुख और सुख को दुःख जाने, वही ज्ञानी है।

२५. यह कलम चार आने को मिलती है।

२६. दो आने को सेर भर जामुन मिलता है।

२७. जिसने अपने मन को नहीं जीता, वह संसार को भला क्या जीतेगा?

से (Instrumental and Ablative Case-sign)

It is the case-sign of both Instrumental (करण) and Ablative (अपादान) cases. When the sense of separation is predominant we have Ablative Case. पेड़ से पत्ते गिरे *Leaves fell from the tree.* But in चाकू से फल काटो *Cut the fruit with a knife,* Knife is in the Instrumental case. The Instrumental से is to be translated by 'by' or 'with' in English. Instrumental has the sense of 'by means of' or simply 'by'.

लड़के से कोई गलती हो जाय तो उसे माफ कर देना चाहिये.

'If any mistake is committed by a boy, he should be pardoned'.

से has also the sense of 'by' in an adverb.

खूब मेहनत से पढ़ो—*'Read laboriously'.*

से is used to denote :—

(1) the instrument.

मैं कलम से लिखता हूं। *I write with a pen.*

मैं सरौते से सुपारी काटता हूँ। *I cut nut by a Sarouta.* (an instrument).

(2) the cause or origin.

आपके आने से मैं बहुत खुश हूं। I am greatly pleased by your coming.

राम मलेरिया से मरा। Ram died of malaria.

गंगा हिमालय से निकलती है। Ganga rises from the Himalaya.

(3) the manner.

एक क्रम से नाम पुकारो। *Call the names in an order.*

तेजी से जाओ। *Go quickly.*

ध्यान से सुनो। *Hear attentively.*

(4) in accompaniment of or association with.

बड़ी तैयारी से विवाह हो रहा है। *The marriage is taking place with great preparations.*

Here से means साथ

मैंने तुमसे ब्याह किया है। *I have married you.*

(5) Change from one condition to another.

क्या से क्या हो गया ? *What has turned into what ?*

वह गरीब से अमीर हो गया। *From poor he became rich.*

(6) Exchange of a thing.

धान से घी बदल कर ले लो।

Exchange ghee by paddy.

(7) Starting point (time or place)

मैं कलकत्ते से आ रहा हूँ। *I am coming from Calcutta.*

कल से होटल में हूँ। *I am in hotel from yesterday.*

मैं सुबह से काम कर रहा हूँ। *I am working from morning.*

(8) Separation or avoidance.

सिर से बाल झरा। *Hair fell from the head.*

छूत से बचो। *Avoid contagion.*

(9) Duration, with the sense of continuity.

मैं चार साल से बनारस में हूँ। *I am at Banaras for four years.*

एक हफ्ते से मैं बीमार हूँ। *I am ill for a week.*

(10) Comparison.

सोना चांदी से कीमती धातु है। *Gold is a more valuable metal than silver.*

वह कक्षा में सबसे तेज विद्यार्थी है। *He is the most brilliant student in (his) class.*

वह मुझसे लम्बा है। *He is taller than I.*

(11) Sense of 'to' in English.

प्रभु से मेरी यही प्रार्थना है। *This is my prayer to God.*

(12) To express need or use.

मुझे इससे क्या काम ? *Of what use is this to me ?*

It also comes after the nominative when the sentence is in passive or impersonal voice.

मुझसे रोटी खाई गई। *The bread was eaten by me.*

मुझसे खाया नहीं जाता। *I cannot eat (literally-eating cannot be done by me.)*

सीता से चला नहीं जाता। *Sītā cannot move or walk. (literally-going cannot be done by Sītā)*

It should be noted that से comes with the 'person object' when कहना, पूछना, बोलना, बकना, बात करना, प्रार्थना करना, बताना and similar verbs come.

राम से जाकर यह सब कहो। *Tell all this to Ram (after going).*

मैं आप से यह पूछना चाहता हूँ। *I want to ask this of you.*

तुमसे बोलने का जी नहीं करता। *I do not like to speak to you.*

मुझसे ज्यादा बहस न करो। *Do not discuss it with me.*

से alone does not represent the full ablative sense of 'out of' in Hindī. For this में से (case-signs of Locative and Ablative) are used together and then they convey the sense of 'out of'. जेब में से पैसे निकाल लो। *Take money (literally-pice) from (out of) (my) pocket.*

घर में से एक पलंग निकालो। *Take a bed out of the room.*

Omission of से

से is sometimes omitted :—

इस तरह से काम करो। *Do this work in this manner.*

मैं आंखों देखी कहता हूँ *I say what I have seen with my eyes.* Here it is आंखों से देखी।

Similarly कानों सुनी is कानों से सुनी।

मैं अपने हाथों काम करता। *I work with my own hands* ; से is omitted after हाथों.

में Locative (अधिकरण)

It is a locative sign, which generally comes in the sense of 'in' 'within' or 'into' and sometimes 'at'.

Presence.

वह घर में रहता है। *He lives in (his) house.*

इस बक्स में इसे रख दो। *Put it into this box.*

Price.

यह पुस्तक मैंने आठ आने में खरीदी है। *I have purchased this book at eight annas.*

यह तुमने कितने में खरीदा ? *At what price did you purchase it ?*

Comparison.

दोनों कपड़ों में मुझे यही पसन्द है। *Between these two cloths I like it.*

सब लड़कों में मोहन तेज है। *Mohan is the most brilliant of all boys.*

Sometimes में is also omitted.

मेरे भाग्य तेरे हाथ है। *My fate is in your hand.*

पर **Locative** (अधिकरण)

It is equivalent to 'at', 'up' or 'upon' in English.

वह अपनी जगह पर है। *He is at his place.*

बनारस गंगातट पर है। *Banaras is on the bank of Ganga.*

किताब मेज पर है। *Book is on the table.*

It also denotes sequence of time or action.

शाम होने पर मैं आऊँगा। *I will come after the evening.*

शिक्षक के न रहने पर कक्षा में हल्ला होता है। *There is some noise* (or *disturbance*) *when the teacher is not in the class.*

It also indicates cause or reason.

झूठ बोलने पर गुस्सा होता है। *One feels anger at speaking lie* ; पर comes to denote period of time or distance.

दो दो घंटे पर दवा खानी होगी। *The medicine is to be taken after every two hours.*

कोस कोस भर पर वहां सराय बनी है। *There is a Sarai after every kos (two miles).*

का Sign of Genitive Possessive Case (सम्बन्ध)

It is equivalent to the English 'of' and has a possessive or genitive sense. Generally it has the sense of 'belonging to' or 'pertaining to', but conveys other forms of relationship also. Its one peculiarity should be observed. It changes into की when the following noun is feminine, either singular or plural, and into के when the following noun is masculine and plural or when an oblique form comes after it.

राम का बेटा, राम की बेटी—Singular

राम के बेटे, राम की बेटियां—Plural

राम के बेटे को बुलाओ and not राम का बेटे को बुलाओ. Here बेटे is not plural but the oblique form of बेटा (because को case-sign is used) राम के बेटों को बुलाओ means 'call Ram's sons' but राम के बेटे को बुलाओ means 'call Ram's son'.

Thus when the following masculine noun has no separate plural form, it is के which is sufficient to denote plurality.

राम के मकान *Ram's houses.*

We have already said that it has possessive sense.

राम का घर *house of Ram*

राम की गाय *cow of Ram*

Mark the place of का or की in Hindī. It comes after the possessor and not the thing possessed as in English.

It also denotes the material of which a thing is made.

सोने की घड़ी *a watch of gold.*

चमड़े का जूता *a shoe of leather.*

In Hindī it has some special uses—it denotes the sense of price or worth and measure of space of time also.

यह दो रुपये की कलम है। *This pen is worth two rupees* or *the price of this pen is two rupees.*

रुपये का दो सेर चावल मिलता है। *Rice is sold at the rate of two seers a rupee.*

यह बड़े काम की चीज हैं। *This is a very useful thing.*

वह नाम का भूखा है। *He hankers after name.*

बेकार क्या घूमते हो ? *Why are (you) wandering uselessly ?*

यह शाम का वक्त है *It is evening time (time of evening).*

यह लूट का माल है *It is a looted property.*

किराये का मकान। *A rented house* or *a house to be given on rent.*

It has also the sense of purpose.

खाने की चीज। *a thing to eat.*

सोने की दवा। *a medicine which brings sleep* or
for the purpose of causing sleep.

खेलने का सामान। *articles for play.*

नहाने का साबुन। *a soap for bathing (a toilet soap).*

पीने का पानी। *Water for drinking.*

पढ़ने का चश्मा। *a reading glass (spectacles).*

धूप का चश्मा *Sun goggles or spectacles for going in sun.*

Mark the following uses of का or की

वह कमाल का आदमी है। *He is a man of qualities.*

वह बेकार का आदमी है। *He is a useless man.*

वह बड़े शान की बात है। *This is of great brilliance.*

वह खेल का मैदान है। *That is a play-ground.*

झूठमूठ का मुझे परेशान न करो। *Don't vex me unnecessarily.*

मोहन का अब क्या कहना ? *What to say of Mohan now ?*

दुःख का मारा हुआ। *Afflicted by troubles.*

गर्मी के मारे परेशान। *Worried by heat.*

सांप का काटा शायद ही बचता है। *Seldom is a snake-bitten man saved.*

जीने का क्या ठिकाना ! *What is the certainty of life !*

सब का यही हाल है। *Everybody's condition is like this.*

जब भाग्य अच्छा होता है तो मिट्टी का सोना हो जाता हैं।
When the fate is good, even dust becomes gold.

फूलों की सेज। *A bed strewn with flowers.*

Use of Two Case Signs Together

में से—It has the sense of 'out of'

इस डाली में से जितने फल चाहो निकाल लो। *Take as many fruits as you like out of this basket.*

घर में से कपड़े निकाल कर धूप में डाल दो। *Take out clothes from the room and spread them in the sun.*

में का—इस डाली में का एक भी आम पका नहीं। *No mango of this basket is ripe.*

पर से—छत पर से कपड़े उठा लाओ। *Bring the clothes from the roof.*

पर के—छत पर के कपड़े सूखने दो। *Let the clothes on the roof dry.*

पर का—टेबुल पर का अखबार मत छूओ। *Don't touch the newspaper on the table.*

Out of the two case-signs coming together, one must be a locative case-sign.

Vocative (सम्बोधन)

The Vocative form is the form of a Noun, denoting a person or a personified object, when it is addressed. It is identical with the oblique form without nasalization.

रे or ओ रे लड़के ! ए or ऐ लड़के ! ओ or ओ रे, लड़के।

री or ओ री, ए लड़की ! री लड़कियां !

There are several words which are used before the Vocative forms.

Tatsama हे, अहो, आये, रे,

Tadbhava and other interjections री, ए, ओ,

Two combined interjections ओ रे, ओ री, एरे, ओरे.

Mark that there is no nasalization in any vocative form, लड़को not लड़कों, लड़कियो (not लड़कियों), भाइयो (not भाइयों), बहनो (not बहनों).

Some writers use the Sanskṛt Vocative forms of Nouns in Hindī also. Thus some write हे प्रभु ! and some हे प्रभो, हे दीनबन्धु, हे दीनबन्धो, हे पिता, हे पितः. Both forms are used in Hindī and should therefore be considered as correct. The use of हे, आर्य etc. is also not necessary, they are sometimes omitted by even standard writers. The use of the sign of interjection (!) is also these days considered unnecessary. Often a comma is used where the sign of interjection would have been more proper. In Sanskṛt form nouns ending in आ the final आ is changed to ए in the vocative as नीरवते from नीरवता, सीते from सीता.*

---

* 'हे प्रभो, ज्ञानदाता ज्ञान मुझको दीजिये'—Pratāp Nārāyaṇ Miśra

विस्मृति आ, अवसाद घेर ले
नीरवते, बस चुप कर दे
चेतनता, चल जा, जड़ा से
आज शून्य मेरा भर दो—Kāmāyanī.
हे सीते ! तुम कहां हो ?
सीता, तू कहां चली गई थी ?

If चेतनता is taken as Vocative here, it should be चेतनते like नीरवते and there should be interjection mark (!) or a comma. There is great laxity in the use of the Vocative form and proper punctuation marks even by standard writers in Hindī.

CHAPTER VII

Pronouns (सर्वनाम)

In Hindī, the pronoun is akin to the English pronoun. The Personal pronouns are divided into three classes, according to three persons and each class has singular and plural forms.

	Singular	*Plural*
First person	मैं I	हम We
Second person	तू Thou	तुम You
Third person	वह He, she, it	वे They

All these pronouns undergo changes in declension. मैं is equivalent to 'I' in English. It is said to be derived from मया in Sanskṛt, the instrumental form of अहम् . हम though considered to be plural is used as singular also, specially in the Eastern parts of Hindī area. It also seems to be derived from अहम् and its derivation sanctions its singular use. तुम is considered by grammarians to be plural, but is used in the singular. It is derived from त्वम् Skt. Thus हम and तुम both are really singulars and to denote plurality लोग is used with हम and तुम. वे is considered also as plural but is alse used as an honorific third person singular pronoun. To denote clear plurality लोग is added to वे also.

Thus, considering the use of these personal pronouns the position is this.

	Singular	*Plural*
I.	मैं, हम	हम लोग
II.	तू , तुम, आप	तुम लोग
III.	वह. वे	वे लोग

आप is an honorific personal pronoun. तू is addressed to a man of inferior status, a servant or child. It is also used in addressing God. It is better to avoid the use of तू unless the speaker is sure about the inferior status of the person addressed to, and for a foreigner it is better to avoid its use, otherwise the person addressed may take offence to its use. तू, तुम, and आप are used taking into consideration the status of the person addressed to. If the man addressed to is an elderly or a respected person or of equal status but without familiarity or acquaintance, आप should be used. Between friends or persons on very intimate terms तुम may be used. Perhaps it is thoughtless to treat तुम as plural. It may be a blind acceptance of English Grammar because 'you', the equivalent of तुम in English, is plural. In Hindī, really हम लोग, तुम लोग and वे लोग are plural personal pronouns. वे आ रहे हैं is '*He is coming*' (if the man is a respectable gentleman) and '*They are coming*' both. Even in case of वे often लोग is added to denote clear plurality. यह and वह should not be used in the plural.

In the Accusative, मैं has two forms मुझे and मुझको. In the genitive मेरा is used, which has its fem. form मेरी and मेरे is the masc. plural form. रा, री, रे may be considered as special case-signs of the genitive (सम्बन्ध) and are used only with personal pronouns. With आप, however, ना, नी, ने, ने is used after आ is shortened to अ— अपना, अपनी, अपने. तू is also declined on the analogy of मैं. Thus we have तुझे and तुझको, तुझसे, तुझमें, तुझ पर and तेरा, तेरी, तेरे in the genitive. हम is declined as हमें, हमको, हममें, हम पर and हमारा, हमारी, हमारे. In the colloquial speech we hear मेरे को and तेरे को for मुझको and तुझको but these forms are not considered elegant. तुम is declined as तुम्हें, तुमको, तुमसे, तुममें, तुमपर and तुम्हारा, तुम्हारी, तुम्हारे.

Declension of the Personal pronouns is given at the end of the Chapter.

It should be noted that while the genitive रा is added to हम after lengthening of the last vowel अ, in तुम्हारा before such lengthening ह comes in (तुम्+ह+आ+रा=तुम्हारा)

Use of सा with Pronouns.

सा is often used with मुझ and तुझ

मुझ-सा गरीब कौन है ? *Who is poor like me ?*

'Like me' should not be translated as मैं सा but 'like you' will be तुम-सा or तुम्ह-सा when the man is of inferior status.

वैसा 'like that' is perhaps formed by वह+सा or वे+सा but now is generally used as meaning 'like' or 'similar.'

The peculiar use of सा with pronouns should be carefully noted.

यह and वह are used as Demonstrative Pronouns also, when there is definite pointing out.

यह तुम्हारी पुस्तक है। This is your book.

वह तुम्हारा मकान है। That house is yours.

आप is also a Reflexive Pronoun (निज वाचक) and is often used with ही. वह आप कहता है कि मैं दोषी हूं *He himself says that he is guilty*. वह आपही हँसता है और आप ही रोता है। *He himself smiles and himself weeps*. A compound word अपने आप is also used in Reflexive sense. This Reflexive आप is different from आप of the second person. मैं आप जाता हूँ *I myself am going*. Here आप is Reflexive pronoun but in आप कहां जाते हैं, आप is Personal. pronoun. In my opinion this use of आप as Reflexive is a special use of आप and should not be considered as pronoun. Use of स्वयं or खुद in its place is growing.

Besides the Personal pronouns the following classes are recognised :—

1. Demonstrative यह, वह
   निश्चयवाचक
2. Reflexive आप
   निजवाचक
3. Indefinite कोई, कुछ
   (अनिश्चयवाचक)
4. Relative जो
   (सम्बन्धवाचक)
5. Interrogative कौन, क्या
   (प्रश्नवाचक)

Declension of Pronouns

The declension of the following pronouns is to be noted :—

	यह		वह	
N.	यह	ये	वह	वे
	इसने	इनने	उसने	उनने
		इन्होंने		उन्होंने
Acc.	इसे	इन्हें	उसे	उन्हें
	इसका	इनको	उसको	उनको
Ins. Abl.	इससे	इनसे	उससे	उनसे
D,	इसको	इनको	उसको	उनको
G.	इसका (की)	इनका (की)	उसका (की)	उनका
L.	इसमें	इनमें	उसमें	उनमें
	इसपर	इनपर	उस पर	उन पर

	जो		कौन	
N.	जो	जो	कौन	कौन
	जिसने	जिनने	किसने	किनने
		जिन्होंने		किन्होंने
Acc.	जिसे	जिन्हें	किसे	किन्हें
	जिसको	जिनको	किसको	किनको
Ins. Abl.	जिससे	जिनसे	किससे	किनसे
D.	जिसको	जिनको	किसको	किनको
G.	जिसका (की)	जिनका (की)	किसका (की)	किनका (की)
L.	जिसमें	जिनमें	किसमें	किनमें
	जिसपर	जिनपर	किसपर	किनपर

N. B. There seems a growing tendency to use इन्होंने and उन्होंने in place of इनने and उनने which are used in poetry.

It is important to note the constructive stem of tbe following pronouns यह, वह, जो and कौन—

	यह	वह	जो	कौन
Nomi. Case.	य	व	ज	क
Oblique Case.	इ	उ	जि	कि

In the Oblique cases स is added to the base. Thus we get the forms इस, उस, जिस, किस. In the plural forms न is added and the forms are इन, उन, जिन, किन.

The suffix तना is added to form pronominal adjectives कितना (कि+तना), इतना, उतना and जितना. Another kind of pronominal adjectives are formed by सा to Vṛddhi वृद्धि forms of the bases of pronouns in oblique cases. Thus we have इ-ऐ+सा=ऐसा उ—वैसा, जि—जैसा, कि—कैसा

The pronoun सो (for 'he') is not considered elegant in modern usage. However, it is nsed as correlative pronoun with जो. This सो should not be used for वह in the beginning of a sentence. Its pronominal base in oblique cases is ति and so we have such forms like तितना and तैसा. तैसा is used in some proverbs as जैसे को तैसा. सो is used by religious preachers using the Pandit style जो है सो. It is, however, not considered to be a happy expression and it is better to avoid it.

In the colloquial, कै is often used for कितने,—कै पैसे दूँ ? How many pice have I to give ? कै लड़के आये हैं How many students have come? कै is used in conversation only and कितने is used in writing.

There is an emphatic affix ई which is added to many pronouns. We have thus such forms as उसी (उस्+ई), किसी (किस्+ई) वही (वह्+ई). In plural ह is added before this emphatic ई, for example उन्+ह्+ईं= उन्हीं, किन्+ह्+ईं=किन्ही.

When a pronoun comes before a noun, the case-sign is used after the noun, otherwise the case-sign immediately follows a pronoun e.g. उस घर में, उस लड़के पर गुस्सा मत करो but उसमें, उसपर गुस्सा मत करो.

From the declension of यह, वह, जो and कौन it will be seen that there are two alternative forms when ने, is used in the Nominative case. इनने, उन्होंने; उनने, उन्होंने; जिनने, जिन्होंने; किनने, किन्होंने. Of these

1. Vṛddhi forms of इ and उ are ए and ऐ.

two forms the latter one are preferred in writing prose and the former forms are often used in conversation or in poetry. Though the grammarians treat इनने, इन्होंने, उनने, उन्होंने etc as plural forms, in fact, they are used as singular for respectable persons. Here also the word लोग or सब is used to denote plural sense उनकी जमीन रामपुर गाँव में है। *His land is in Rampur village* उन लोगों की जमीन रामपुर गांव में है। *Their land is in Rampur village.*

कौन refers ordinarily to a person and क्या to a thing. कौन आया है ? *Who has come* ? क्या आया है ? *What has come* ? But often कौन is also used, where perhaps क्या is more appropriate. कौन चीज तुम खरीदोगे ? and क्या चीज तुम खरीदोगे ? has almost the same meaning *'Which thing would you purchase'* ? and *'What thing would you purchase ?'* कुछ has the sense of some, any, some thing, anything. कुछ refers to a thing, which may be counted or weighed. It is also used in a collective sense कुछ घी चाहिये। कुछ बातें मुझे पसन्द नहीं हैं। कुछ लड़के आये थे। कुछ पानी बरसा है। कुछ पैसे मुझे चाहिये। *Some ghee is wanted. I do not like something. Some boys have come. There was a little rain I want some money* (literally 'pice'). Mark the difference in the meaning of कुछ.

We have already noted that आप is really a honorific second person singular pronoun. The peculiarity about its use is that a plural verb is used in the sentences when it is the subject आप कहते हैं। *You say;* आप दिन में कहा रहते हैं ? *Where do you live in the day ?* हैं and थे (and not है or था) is used after आप. In the Genitive singular the affix रा is not used with आप. The first vowel of आप is shortened and ना is added आप-अप-अपना (अपनी, अपने).

The word आप is said to be derived from Skt. आत्मन्. Perhaps this ना is an influence of न् of आत्मन्. A pronoun is not used as a noun, but अपना is an exception. Perhaps it is because अपना is derived from आत्मन्, a noun in Sanskṛt. In the sentence जब अपनों से मदद न मिली तो दूसरों का क्या भरोसा ? *When no help was received from one's own people what trust may be placed upon others ?* अपना has अपनी and अपने as the Genitive feminine and plural forms.

मैं and तू take special forms मे and ते in the Genitive case before genitive suffix रा is added. Thus we have मेरा (not मैं रा) and तेरा and (not तू रा) in the genitive.

Combination of Pronouns

Hindī has a peculiarity in the use of compound pronouns. Sometimes a pronoun is repeated to give a special meaning to it- कोई कोई ऐसा कहते हैं। *Some say like this;* कौन कौन जाना चाहता है ? *Who wants to go ?* मैं किन-किनकी बातें सुनूँ ? *Whose talks am I to hear ?* Two different pronouns may also combine with one another. जो कोई, जिस किसी को, जो कुछ. There is another form of combination where न intervenes between two pronouns of the same kind कुछ न कुछ, कोई न कोई।

N. B. In my opinion कुछ and कोई are not really speaking pronouns. कोई is said to be derived from कोऽपि Skt. which itself is a combination of कः and अपि. कः is a pronoun but अपि is indeclinable. कुछ is perhaps derived from कश्चित्. It is more of an adjective than a pronoun. According to Guru there are eleven pronouns in Hindī. They are मैं, तू, आप, यह, वह, सो, जो, कोई, कुछ, कौन, क्या. Of these we have to examine the nature of सो, कोई, कुछ, क्या. We have already commented upon the use of सो in modern Hindī. कोई according to the derivation is not a simple but a compound pronoun. कुछ is more an adjective than pronoun. कुछ combines with एक and we get कुछेक (कुछ+एक). A pronoun may also be combined with सा e.g. कौन-सा, तुम-सा etc.

Declension of Personal Pronouns

	Singular	*Plural*
	मैं I	**हम We**
Nom.	में, मैंने I	हम, हमने We
Accus.	मुझको, मुझे To me	हमको, हमें To us
Instr. } Abl. }	मुझसे By me	हमसे By us
Dat.	मेरे लिये For me	हमारे लिये For us
Gen.	मेरा, मेरी, मेरे My, mine	हमारा, हमारी, हमारे Our
Loc.	मुझमें, मुझ पर In me, On me	हममें, हम पर In us, On us

	तू **Thou**	तुम **You**
Nom.	तू , तूने Thou	तुम, तुमने You
Acc.	तुझको, तुझे To thee	तुमको, तुम्हें To you
Instr. / Abl.	तुझसे By thee	तुमसे By you
Dat.	तेरे लिए For thee	तुम्हारे लिए For you
Gen.	तेरा, तेरी, तेरे Thine	तुम्हारा, तुम्हारी, तुम्हारे Your, Your's
Loc.	तुझमें, तुझ पर in thee, on thee	तुम में, तुम पर in you, on you

	वह **He, She, It**	वे **They**
Nom.	वह, उसने He, She	वे, उन्होंने, उनने[1] They
Acc.	उसको, उसे To him	उनको, उन्हें To them
Instr. / Abl.	उससे By him, her	उनसे By them
Dat.	उसके लिए For him, her	उनके लिए For them
Gen.	उसका, उसकी, उसके His her	उनका, उनकी, उनके Their
Loc.	उसमें, उस पर In him, her, on him, on her	उनमें, उनपर In them, at them

	आप **Honorific for 'you'**
Nom.	आप, आपने You
Acc.	आपको To you
Instr. / Abl.	आपसे By you
Dat.	आपके लिए For you
Gen.	आपका, आपकी, आपके Your
Loc.	आपमें आप पर In you, on you.

---

1. उनने and इनने are generally used in colloquial language or in poetry.

CHAPTER VIII

Adjective

There are two kinds of adjectives in Hindī, one inflected and the other uninflected. The inflected adjective changes on account of gender and person of a noun qualified by it. Thus बढ़िया which is an uninflected adjective, is neither affected by gender nor by person. बढ़िया धोतियां, बढ़िया मकान, बढ़िया घड़ी. But inflected adjective अच्छा has its fem. form अच्छी e. g. अच्छा लड़का and अच्छी लड़की. A large number of Sanskṛt adjectives are used in Hindī. In Hindī it is not necessary to use the fem. from of adjective when the word qualified is feminine. सुन्दर बालक and सुन्दरी बालिका both are correct and in Hindī it is not necessary to write सुन्दरी (fem. form of सुन्दर). In Sanskṛt both the adjective and the substantive should be of the same gender. In Hindī the observance of this rule in case of feminine words makes the style highly pedantic and artificial. सुन्दर स्त्री is quite good and elegant Hindī. A masc. noun in no case should be qualified by a fem. adjective as उत्तमा पुरुष or अच्छी लड़का would be most offensive. There are quite a large number of tadbhava or non-Sanskṛt adjectives which have their fem. forms. Where there are fem. forms they must be used with fem. nouns. Thus अच्छा, अच्छी काला, काली, पीला, पीली etc must be used taking into consideration the gender of the noun. It shows that the peculiarity about the use of adjectives in Hindī is that some adjectives have both masc. and fem. forms and some have only one form.

An inflected adjective in its masc. form undergoes change in the last vowel, when the noun qualified, is in one of the oblique cases. The last vowel आ is changed to ए. Where ने is used in the noun, this rule is observed काले लड़के ने मुझसे कहा। is the correct form and not काला लड़के ने or काला लड़का ने. This peculiarity in the use of inflected adjective (mostly tadbhava) should be carefully observed, otherwise the language would be faulty or ridiculous.

All numeral adjectives ending in वाँ like पाँचवाँ, सातवाँ have their corresponding fem. and oblique forms such as पाँचवीं and पाँचवें. They are inflected like काला, काली and काले.

The use of सा (सी, से) also deserve to be noted. It indicates resemblance and is often used with adjectives, as, छोटा-सा घर, लम्बा-सा आदमी, छोटी-सी टोपी, बड़ी-सी किताब. Sometimes सा (सी, से) comes after the genitive case-sign as लड़के की-सी बोली, घोड़े का-सा मुँह, लड़के की-सी बोली really means *'the speech like that of the speech of a boy'* though literally *'it is the speech like that of a boy'* घोड़े का-सा मुँह *'face like that of the face of a horse'*, though literally it is *'face like that of a horse.'* Sometimes the genitive case-sign is omitted घोड़े-सा मुँह, लड़के-सी बोली it would be similar to the expression *'horse-like face'* or *'boy-like speech'*. सा has the sense of *'almost like'* and not *'fully like.'*

सा or सी denotes intensity at some places. In such expressions मैं बहुत-सा खा गया or जरा-सा भी नहीं खा सका we have a peculiar use of सा. In conversation such expressions are very common and their use may baffle a non-Hindī speaker. थोड़ा-सा घी लाओ *'bring a little ghee'* and not *'bring little-like ghee.* This peculiarity in the use of सा has no parallel in English.

A large number of Sanskṛt adjectives are used only in mas. form. Some writers adopt the Sanskṛt mode of using Sanskṛt adjectives and they use Sanskṛt fem. adj. before fem. Sanskṛt nouns. This is more seen in poetry. Specially in Priyapravās—a famous poetical work which is full of such expressions; गुणवती युवती बहु बालिका. But this is not the common style of Hindī and is just an influence of Sanskṛt syntax.

Adjectives may be classified under the following heads .—

1. Pronominal (सार्वनामिक) 2. Qualitative (गुणवाचक) and 3. Numerical (संख्यावाचक)

Almost all pronouns may be used as adjectives when they qualify nouns following them.

यह आदमी *This man* वह लड़का *That boy*	Demonstrative Pronoun.
कौन औरत ? *Which woman ?* क्या जरूरत ? *What need ?*	Interrogative Pronoun.
कोई लड़का *Any boy* कुछ आम *Some mangoes*	Indefinite Pronoun.
जो लोग *Those people*	Relative Pronoun.

In the sentence किसी को बुलाओ *'Call any body'* किसी is a pronoun but in the sentence किसी विद्यार्थी को बुलाओ *'Call any student'* किसी is a pronominal adjective, because किसी is followed by विद्यार्थी. At the above places, in fact, pronouns have been used as adjectives.

A Qualitative adjective may describe the condition of a thing or its quality as हरा, दुबला, भला, बुरा, बीमार, अच्छा, ठंडा, चिकना etc.

There are some Hindī adjectives ending in आ which have no corresponding fem. forms, as घटिया, बढ़िया, उम्दा, दुखिया.

Numeral adjectives are of different kinds. They may indicate definite number as एक, दो, चार or indicate an indefinite number as कम, अधिक etc. They may also indicate the quantity of a thing as कम, ज्यादा अधिक, आधा etc.

इस क्लास में कम लड़के हैं। *There are a few students in this class.* Here कम indicates number. But कम घी खाया करो। *Take (eat) little ghee.* Here कम indicates smallness in quantity.

We shall treat the topic of numerals separately as, there are several peculiar formations in Hindī from words indicating number.

Some peculiarities regarding the use of adjectives.

1. Case-sign is attached to a noun qualified by an adjective and the adjective ending in आ takes the oblique form.

पुराने लोगों की बातें नये लड़कों को अच्छी नहीं लगतीं,
'Modern (new) boys do not like the talks of old people.'

Here पुराना and नया will be incorrect..........Use of oblique form पुराने and नये is necessary.

2. Adjectives, other than those ending in आ, do not change in the feminine.

Thus we have adjectives like लाल, सर्द, गर्म, तेज which qualify both mas. and fem. nouns.

लाल कुर्ता, लाल कुर्ती
सर्द मौसम, सर्द हवा
गर्म पानी, गर्म हवा
तेज़ लड़का, तेज़ लड़की

The sense of comparative and superlative degree is expressed generally by the use of proper case-signs से or को after that with which the comparison is made.

Comparative Degree By use of से

मोहन राम से लम्बा है। *Mohan is taller than Ram.*

राधे सोहन से छोटा है। *Radhe is smaller than Sohan.*

गंगा यमुना से लम्बी है। *Gangā is longer than Yamunā.*

Superlative Degree

शीला क्लास में सबसे सुन्दर लड़की है *Shīlā is the most beautiful girl in the class.*

वह सबसे तेज़ लड़का है। *He is the most brilliant boy.*

Thus when there is comparison between two things, से is only used but when comparison is made with all things of any class. सब is used with से to give superlative sense.

For से in literary Hindī, अपेक्षा is also used—मोहन राम की अपेक्षा लम्बा ह।

By use of में

में is also used to denote superiority of a thing when compared with two or more things.

Comparative Degree

वह दोनों में सुखी है। *He is the happier of the two.*

Superlative Degree

वह सबसे अच्छा है। *He is best of all.*

Thus it is clear that in Hindī (Tadbhava) we do not use special suffixes as in English to denote the comparative and superlative degrees. Thus we have no comparative or superlative forms of सुखी and अच्छा. Only in case of some Sanskṛt words, special comparative and superlative forms are used.

	Comparative	*Superlative*
महत्	महत्तर	महत्तम
बृहत्	बृहत्तर	बृहत्तम
प्रिय	प्रियतर	प्रियतम
सुन्दर	सुन्दरतर	सुन्दरतम
कठिन	कठिनतर	कठिनतम
लघु	लघुतर	लघुतम

There are many superlative forms of Sanskṛt words, which are used to denote simply the sense of superiority. श्रेष्ठ and उत्तम, though superlative in form, are generally used, when the intention is not necessarily to convey superlative sense. To give definite superlative sense सर्व is added to some of such words श्रेष्ठ—सर्वश्रेष्ठ, उत्तम—सर्वोत्तम.

The following comparative and superlative forms are also sometimes used :—

ज्येष्ठ	ज्येष्ठतर	ज्येष्ठतम
श्रेष्ठ	श्रेष्ठतर	श्रेष्ठतम
उत्कृष्ट	उत्कृष्टतर	उत्कृष्टतम

Sometimes कम or ज्यादा (अधिक) are also used before an adjective when comparison is intended.

मलमल खद्दर से कम टिकाऊ होता है। *Muslin is less durable than Khaddar.*

मिट्टी के मकान से ईंट का मकान ज्यादा मजबूत होता है। *A house made of bricks is stronger than a house of clay.*

See that 'stronger' is denoted by use of two words ज्यादा मजबूत.

Use of Adjectives as Nouns.

Many adjectives in Hindī are used as nouns.

छोटे-बड़े सभी यही कहते हैं। *All big and small persons say this*

Here छोटे-बड़े is adjective qualifying 'unexpressed' आदमी but they have been used as nouns.

अमीर, गरीब, गोरा and other such words are used as nouns also.

अमीरों की बात ही क्या ? *What to speak of the rich* (persons) ?

गरीबों पर दया करो। *Be merciful to the poor people.*

बहुतों को यह भी पता नहीं। *Many people do not even know this.*

झूठों पर कोई विश्वास नहीं करता। *No body believes liars.*

CHAPTER IX

Numerals (संख्यावाचक)

Numeral words may be classed as (1) Cardinal (गणनावाचक) (2) Ordinal (क्रमवाचक) and (3) Multiplicatives (आवृत्तिवाचक).

Cardinal numbers are for counting. Hindi cardinals are given below :—

1	एक	26	छब्बीस	51	इक्यावन	76	छिहत्तर
2	दो	27	सत्ताइस	52	बावन	77	सतहत्तर
3	तीन	28	अट्ठाइस	53	तिरपन	78	अठहत्तर
4	चार	29	उन्तीस	54	चौवन	79	उन्यासी
5	पाँच	30	तीस	55	पचपन	80	अस्सी
6	छः	31	इकतीस	56	छप्पन	81	इक्यासी
7	सात	32	बत्तीस	57	सत्तावन	82	बयासी
8	आठ	33	तैंतीस	58	अट्ठावन	83	तिरासी
9	नौ	34	चौंतीस	59	उनसठ	84	चौरासी
10	दस	35	पैंतीस	60	साठ	85	पचासी
11	ग्यारह	36	छत्तीस	61	इकसठ	86	छियासी
12	बारह	37	सैंतीस	62	बासठ	87	सत्तासी
13	तेरह	38	अड़तीस	63	तिरसठ	88	अठ्ठासी
14	चौदह	39	उनचालिस	64	चौसठ	89	नवासी
15	पन्द्रह	40	चालिस	65	पैंसठ	90	नब्बे
16	सोलह	41	इकतालिस	66	छासठ	91	इकानबे
17	सत्तरह	42	बयालिस	67	सड़सठ	92	बानबे
18	अठारह	43	तैंतालिस	68	अड़सठ	93	तिरानबे
19	उन्नीस	44	चौवालिस	69	उनहत्तर	94	चौरानवे
20	बीस	45	पैंतालिस	70	सत्तर	95	पंचानबे
21	इक्कीस	46	छियालिस	71	इकहत्तर	96	छानबे
22	बाईस	47	सैंतालिस	72	बहत्तर	97	सत्तानबे
23	तेईस	48	अड़तालिस	73	तिहत्तर	98	अन्ठानबे
24	चौबीस	49	उनचास	74	चौहत्तर	99	निनानबे
25	पच्चीस	50	पचास	75	पचहत्तर	100	सौ

Some optional forms are also in use. There is still no standardization of the spelling or pronunciation of these cardinals. They have their local variations also. Some of the optional forms are given below :—

छः, छह,* बाइस, तेईस, चौआलिस, अड़तालिस, चौअन, सँड़सठ, सतसठ, अँड़सठ, उन्नासी .

सुन्ना, शून्य 0.

100 सौ, 200 दो सौ, 300 तीन सौ and so on. 1000 हज़ार, 10000 दस हजार, Million दस लाख, ten millions करोड़, अरब, 1000000000, खरब 100000000000.

After one hundred (एक सौ), the number is simply added to एक सौ as 145 एक सौ पैंतालिस and similarly numbers are added to one thousand and one lakh.

These numbers are used in the same form in both genders.

Fractions.

$\frac{1}{4}$ चौथाई, पाव (to denote weight or distance as पाव भर, पाव कोस)

$\frac{1}{2}$ आधा, अद्धा

$\frac{1}{3}$ तिहाई

$\frac{3}{4}$ पौन, पौना, पौन सेर is $\frac{3}{4}$ of a seer (a measure) but पौन is changed to पौने after $1\frac{3}{4}$, $2\frac{3}{4}$ and so on so $1\frac{3}{4}$ is पौने दो $2\frac{3}{4}$ पौने तीन , पौन literally means 'one quarter less.'

$1\frac{1}{4}$ सवा

$1\frac{1}{2}$ डेढ़

$1\frac{3}{4}$ पौने दो

---

* Some writers write it as छह and छः In my opinion it should be written as छः. ह is seldom pronounced and (:) Visarga is not foreign to Hindī. See छिः. The words छठ, छठी also support the view that it is छः and not छह.

$2\frac{1}{4}$ सवा दो $3\frac{1}{4}$ सवा तीन and so on. Also सवा दो सौ is 225, 325 सवा तीन सौ, सवा पांच हजार is 5250, सवा सात लाख is 725000.

$2\frac{1}{2}$ अढ़ाई, ढाई, अढ़ाई सौ is 250.

$3\frac{1}{2}$ साढ़े तीन, साढ़े चार and so on. Also साढ़े तीन सौ is 350 and साढ़े पाँच हजार is 5500, साढ़े सात लाख is 750000.

Some numerals are combined to show approximation. दो-एक, दो-चार, तीन-चार, चार-पाँच, पाँच-सात, दस-पाँच, पचास-साठ ।

There is no fixed rule for such combinations, but they are combined according to some kind of order. Seldom we get combinations like सात-दस, तेरह-पन्द्रह, सत्तरह-बीस. These combination are made according to usage.

Repetition of numerals

Repetition denotes *'at a time.'*

दो दो लड़के साथ आते हैं *Two boys come at a time.*

एक एक आदमी टिकट कटावें *One man at a time should take a ticket (from a booking office).*

चार-चार कोस पर एक सराय बनी है *There is a Sarai built at every four Kos* (about 2 miles).

Sense of aggregation :—ओं is added to दो and तीन in this sense.

दोनों both, तीनों all three.

With other cardinals also ओं is added to denote the sense of aggregation. चारों (चार+ओं) पाँचों, छओं सातों, आंठों, नओं, दसों and so on. They mean *'all the four'*, *'all the six'* and so on.

This ओं is added to some nouns also in the sense when a large and indefinite number or quantity is to be denoted as बरसों, महीनों, मनों, सेरों, ढेरों, गाड़ियों.

First पहला, Second दूसरा, Third तीसरा, Fourth चौथा. From fifth पाँचवाँ onwards वाँ is the suffix to form ordinals. छठवाँ, सातवाँ,

आठवाँ, नवाँ and onwards. Mark that there is an optional form छठा for छठवाँ. In नवाँ, वाँ is added to न. These have their few forms also by changing the last vowel into ई.

N. B. The Sanskṛt ordinals प्रथम, द्वितीय, तृतीय etc. are also used in literary Hindī. The Skt. ordinals upto tenth is as follows:— प्रथम, द्वितीय, तृतीय, चतुर्थ, पञ्चम, षष्ठ, सप्तम, अष्टम, नवम, दशम.

Names of Hindī dates according to Hindū Calendar.

1. परिवा	2 दूज	3 तीज	4 चौथ	5 पंचमी
6. छठ	7 सप्तमी	8 अष्टमी	9 नवमी	10 दसमी
11 एकादसी	12 दुआदसी	13 तेरस	14 चौदस	15 पूनो, पूरनमासी

(15th date of bright half of the month) and अमावस (the 15th date of the dark half)

N. B. All these words are feminine.

The Sanskṛt dates are also often used. They are प्रतिपदा, द्वितीया, तृतीया, चतुर्थी, पंचमी, षष्ठी, सप्तमी, अष्टमी, नवमी, दशमी, एकादशी, द्वादशी, त्रयोदशी, चतुर्दशी and पूर्णिमा, अमावस्या.

(ला) is a suffix denoting 'position', which is added to some words पह्+ला, अग+ला fore पिछला, back मँझला middle etc.

Multiplicatives (आवृत्तिवाचक)

गुना, the multiplicative suffix, denoting the sense of—'times' in English, is added to numerals.

This is added to slightly modified forms of numerals upto eight. दुगुना or twice, तिगुना thrice, चौगुना four times, पँचगुना five times, छगुना six times सतगुना, seven times and eight times अठगुना. Above that number गुना is added to numerals.

गुना is added to सवा $1\frac{1}{4}$, डेढ़ $1\frac{1}{2}$, अढ़ाई $2\frac{1}{2}$, etc.

हरा is another suffix which is added in the sense of 'fold' इकहरा one-fold or single दुहरा two-fold, तिहरा three-fold, चौहरा four-fold.

सवाया or सवाई is $1\frac{1}{4}$ times.

ड्योढ़ा 1½ are special forms.

इकाई, दहाई, सैकड़ा—In numeration these units of one (इकाई), of ten (दहाई), and hundred सैकड़ा are used.

Numerals having restricted use.

In playing cards the following numerals are used :—

दुग्गी	Card	indicating	number	2
तिग्गी	,,	,,	,,	3
चौआ	,,	,,	,,	4
पंजा	,,	,,	,,	5
छक्का	,,	,,	,,	6
सत्ता	,,	,,	,,	7
अट्ठा	,,	,,	,,	8
नहला	,,	,,	,,	9
दहला	,,	,,	,,	10

1. Mark that the modified form of numerals also occur in cardinals. दु is modified form of दो, ति of तीन, चौ of चार, पँच of पाँच, सत of सात, अठ of आठ.

२. इक is the modified form of एक, दह of दस and सै of सौ. नहला, दहला—here ला is the suffix as in पहला.

The modified forms of these cardinal numerals in words indicating fractions of the coins and some measures are given below, as they often occur in common speech.

इकन्नी 1 anna piece, दुअन्नी 2 anna piece

चवन्नी 4 anna piece, अठन्नी 8 anna piece

अधन्नी is ½ anna piece.

Fraction of a maund (मन)

पाव is quarter seer (सेर)

पौआ a weight of a quarter seer.

आध पाव $\frac{1}{8}$ seer.

अधपई a weight of $\frac{1}{8}$

छटाँक $\frac{1}{16}$ seer

छटंकी a weight of $\frac{1}{16}$ seer

अढ़ैया a weight of $2\frac{1}{2}$ seer

पसेरी a weight of 5 seers

दससेरी (धारा) a weight of 10 seers

आधमन (दो धारा) a weight of 20 seers.

N. B.—The Government of India has recently introduced the Decimal system of coinage and the Metric system of weights and measures, but several of our phrases and idioms based on numerical words have already entered into the very body of our language, and they are part of the living speech.

In Hindī there are various formations from numericals. For example, छठ is a festival falling on the sixth day, छठा is sixth and छठी is a rite or ceremony after the sixth day of the birth of a child.

बरही is a ceremony on the twelfth day after child-birth. But तेरही, though a word formed on the analogy of बरही, is the thirteenth day after the death of the deceased, on which some special rites are performed. तेरस is the thirteenth day of any fortnight. सोरही is however a kind of gamble, played by cowries.

Thus दहाई, is ten-times, दहला is 10-number playing card and दसईं is tenth day on which a special funeral ceremony is observed and दसमी (दशमी) is the tenth day of a month.

Numerals in names

In Hindī area many names are based on words indicating number हजारी प्रसाद, लाखूराम, पदुमलाल, करोड़ीमल etc.

Names like छकौड़ी, तिनकौड़ी (6–cowries, 3–cowries) are also met with.

————

SECTION II

VERB AND CONJUGATION

CHAPTER X

Verb and its root

Formation of Verbs.

A verbal root is that basic form which remains unchanged in the various formations of the verb. Thus पढ़्√पठ् is a verbal root which assumes different forms as पढ़ा (पढ्+आ), पढ़े (पढ्+ए) पढ़ेगा (पढ्+ए+गा), पढ़ता (पढ्+अ+ता) etc. According to some scholars roots like पढ़् end in consonart, as पठ् in Sanskṛt. There are some roots in Hindī which end in a vowel as खा, गा, पी, दे, रो etc. Some scholars however hold that in Hindī there is no root ending in a consonant. According to them पढ़, चल, सुन and कह are roots and not पढ्, चल्, सुन् and कह्. In my opinion in Hindī we have consonantal roots and therefore पढ्, चल्, सुन्, and कह् are such roots. The forms पढ़, चल, सुन and कह are verbal stems, and not verbal roots. Those who hold that पढ़, चल, सुन and कह are vowel ending roots, agree that the last अ in these words is not pronounced. This inherent अ is not pronounced and in the rules of Sandhi, applicable to purely Hindī words, it is seen that this अ is not taken into consideration.* Thus चलूँ is चल्+ऊँ, चलो is चल्+ओ। चल्+ऊँ cannot be चलूँ and चल्+ओ cannot be चलो।

The consonantal roots take अ before adding ना to form verbal noun पढ़ना (पढ़्+अ+ना) लिखना (लिख्+अ+ना). For simplication, we may say that a verbal noun is formed by adding to the stem of a root ending in a consonant. Thus चल is verbal stem (the verbal root being चल्) and ना is added to form verbal noun चलना.† Thus a stem is obtained by detaching ना from the infinitive form of verbs (चल from चलना, सुन from सुनना, कह from कहना etc).

---

* हरेक=हर्+एक, कुछेक=कुछ्+एक

† This ना is a development of नं suffix in Sanskṛt, according to philologists. Thus मरना, पढ़ना, कहना are from मरणं, पठनं and कथनं.

There are two kinds of roots in Hindī :

1. Roots ending in a consonant as पढ्, चल्, कह् etc.
2. Roots ending in a vowel आ, ई, ऊ, ए, ओ as

आ —	आ, गा, जा
ई—	सी, पी, जी
ऊ—	छू, चू, जू
ए—	दे, ले
ओ—	को, रो, सो

A consonantal root is also called "closed root" and a vowel-ending root is called "open root".

A verb in its verbal noun form is ordinarily found and this form is given as verb-form in Hindī dictionaries. Thus पढ़ना and सुनना are really verbal nouns (as they are developed from पठनं and श्रवणं in Sanskṛt) but they are treated as verbs and equivalents of *"to read"* and *"to hear"*. In Hindī पढ़ना and लिखना *"to write"* are also very commonly used as nouns मैं पढना-लिखना नहीं जानता *I do not know to read or write,* or literally, *I do not know reading or writing.* Thus पढ़ना and लिखना may be both a noun or a verb and the reader should be careful to see if it is a noun or a verb at a particular place in a sentence. पढ़ना and लिखना, when noun, should be translated in English as reading and writing. (2)

Roots may further be classified as (1) monosyllabic (एकाक्षरी) (2) bisyllabic (द्वयक्षरी) and (3) tri-syllabic (त्र्यक्षरी). According to this classification जा, गा, छू, दे and ले are monosyllabic, चल्, जल्, सुन् and लिख् are bisyllabic and पकड़्, बिखर्, परोस्, निकल् are tri-syllabic roots. A root may be productive or non-productive. There

(1) A large number of roots in Hindī are derived from Sanskṛt roots as पढ्—पठ्, कह्—कथ् चल्—चर्. Many roots in Hindī are derived from Sanskṛt words by various processes. जा is derived from या (याति) but आ seems to be derived from आयाति by taking its initial letter आ only. रो is from रुद् which takes रो form from its, initial letter रो in रोदति, रोदन etc.

are some roots from which other verbal roots have grown and some roots are unproductive or barren.*

Hoernle was the first linguist who made a study of Hindī roots. पढ़् is a consonantal root and it is transitive but पढ़ा which is a growth of the root पढ़् is different in meaning. पढ़् is *"read"* and पढ़ा is *"teach"*. पढ़ा is a vowel-ending root. The object of पढ़् is an inanimate object and the object of पढ़ा may be either animate or inanimate object. This would be clear from the following examples :—

मैं पुस्तक पढ़ता हूँ *I read a book.*

मैं राम को पढ़ाता हूँ *I teach Ram.*

मैं रामायण पढ़ाता हूँ *I teach Ramayan.*

Thus उठना and उठाना and पढ़ना and पढ़ाना and also उठवाना and पढ़वाना are all not independent verbs. So, उठ्, उठा and उठवा and similarly पढ़्, पढ़ा and पढ़वा are co-related. In this way उठ् and पढ़् are productive roots which produce उठा, उठवा and पढ़ा and पढ़वा. In Hindī the intransitive and transitive forms of a root are co-related* in form, though there may be slight difference in meaning. मर् (मरना) *'die'* and मार् (मारना) *'beat'* have different meanings. वह मरता है *He dies,* वह मारता है *He beats.* A large number of roots like जा (जाना), डाल् (डालना), रह् (रहना), दे (देना) are used as auxiliary roots, but the use of these roots with the main roots makes quite a difference in meaning. Thus वह मारता है is *'He beats'* but वह मार डालता है is *'He kills'*.

We have already said that the form of a verb in Hindī is arrived at by adding ना at the end of a root, as सोना, चूना, लेना, खाना etc. In case of consonantal roots अ is added to the roots before this ना. There are some nouns also, in which the last letter is ना and they are to be distinguished from the verbs. For example सोना is gold (being derived from स्वर्ण Skṛt, and चूना is lime (being derived

---

*. A root is non-productive in the sense that it does not produce another verbal root. A root produces other forms of a word such as noun, adjective etc.

from चूर्ण Skṛt.) The verbs सोना and चूना are formed by adding ना to सो and चू.

Tense in Hindī (काल)

Hindī has also three tenses.—Past, Present and Future, like other languages. Every action or state, according to Kellog, may be conceived of under three different aspects relating to its own progress i.e. (1) as not yet begun, (2) as begun but not completed and (3) as completed. Broadly speaking they correspond with the future, present and past tenses. Again, according to him, there are fifteen tenses, which he has placed in three groups. As the classification of Kellog is very useful and is reasonable, we have adopted it generally.[1]

Group I.—Tenses from the Root

1. Contingent future. 2. Absolute future. 3. Imperative (future).

,, *II.* Tenses from the Imperfect Participle.

1. Indefinite Imperfect
2. Present ,,
3. Past ,,
4. Contingent ,,
5. Presumptive ,,
6. Past Contingent ,,

,, *III.—Tenses from the Perfect Participle*

1. Indefinite Perfect
2. Present ,,
3. Past ,,
4. Contingent ,,
5. Presumptive ,,
6. Past Contingent ,,

---

1. "The above arrangement and nomenclature differs somewhat from any given in earlier Hindī or Hindustānī grammars; but it is believed to rest on sound philosophical principles, and to give a more precise expression to the distinctive characteristics and mutual relations of the several tenses." Kellog—p. 228.

From the above it will be seen that the tenses of Group I are formed from Roots and the tenses of Group II and Group III are formed by Participles. These groups have some common distinctive features.

For conjugation of verbs in Hindī, it is necessary to know the formation of Imperfect and Perfect Participles.

1. The Imperfect Participle is formed by adding ता to the root : डरता (डर्+अ+ता), मिलता (मिल्+अ+ता), कहता (कह्+अ+ता) (Remember that in consonantal root अ is added to form the stem. We may also say that ता is added to the verbal stem डर+ता, मिल+ता, सो+ता and पी+ता etc.)

2. The Perfect Participle is formed by adding आ to the root पढ़्+आ=पढ़ा, कह्+आ=कहा (Remember that if a root ends in आ or ओ, य् is inserted before आ is added.)

ला+य्+आ=लाया, बो+य्+आ=बोया[1]

If a root ends in ई it is shortened before य् is inserted.

पी—पि+य्+आ=पिया, सी—सि+य्+आ=सिया

There are a few roots ending in ऊ—as चू, छू, here ऊ is shortened.

चू—चुआ, छू—छुआ।

(Now the old forms चुवा and छुवा are being discarded. Though according to Sandhi rules of Sanskṛt इ is substituted to य and उ to व and so चुवा and छुवा forms are phonetically sound, the modern writers prefer चुआ and छुआ forms)

We give below some examples of Imperf. Past and Perf. Past, forms of verbs. Their fem. and oblique forms are also given. Sing. forms are given in brackets. Their plural forms are obtained by nasalizing the last vowel ई—सुनी sing, सुनीं plur.

---

1. In verbal forms यी is often optionally written as ई; thus बोयी, गयी are optionally written as बोई, गई।

Stem	*Imperf. Past*	*Perfect Past*	*Oblique Mas.*
सुन	—सुनता (ती)	सुना (सुनी)	सुनते
पढ़	—पढ़ता (ती)	पढ़ी (पढ़ी)	पढ़ते
चल	—चलता (ती)	चला (चली)	चलते
ला	—लाता (ती)	लाया (यी)	लाते
खा	—खाता (ती)	खाया (यी)	खाते
पी	—पीता (ती)	पिया (यी)	पीते
जी	—जीता (ती)	जिया (यी)	जीते
सी	—सीता (ती)	सिया (यी)	सीते
खो	—खोता (ती)	खोया (यी)	खोते
बो	—बोता (ती)	बोया (यी)	बोते

Thus we see that the Participles ता and आ are inflected as ए and ई is changed to ईं in plural. Ex. पीती is Sing. and पीतीं is Plur. सोती is Sing., सोतीं Plur.

The Participle forms like पढता, पढ़ा, पढ़े and पढ़ी may be used as adjectives with or without हुआ. When हुआ (Past Perf. form of हो) it is also inflected like tadbhava adjectives ending in आ.

Conjugation of Verbs

The conjugation of Hindī verbs is simple and regular, except, in case of the following five verbs.

हो	be	हुआ	been.
कर	do	किया	done.
दे	give	दिया	given.
ले	take	लिया	taken.
जा	go	गया	gone.

Thus it may be said that roots हो, कर, दे, ले, जा take special forms हु, कि, दि, लि, ग before perf. part. are added.

So, in all 15 tenses are formed in Hindī. They have been grouped in three groups on the basis of their construction and special features. Of these 15 tenses, three are formed by the root and the remaining twelve by participles, combined, in all the tenses, but two, with an auxiliary verb (Kellog. p. 222).

Hindī also has 3 tenses— Present, Past and Future but these three are of several varieties. So, in all there are 15 tenses. Here we use the word 'tense' in a general sense. These include the moods also of English Grammar.

The distinction of Number and Gender is generally maintained. However the distinction of Gender is not found in the Contingent Future and the Imperative. Everywhere the second and third person sing. terminations are same and the first and third person plural terminations are also same.

Group I.—Tenses of the Future.

(सम्भाव्य भविष्यत्)

1. *Contingent Future.*

	Terminations		चल्		Pronouns	
	S	P	S	P	S	P
1.	ऊँ	एँ	चलूँ	चलें	मैं	वह
2.	ए	ओ	चले	चलो	तू	तुम
3.	ए	एँ	चले	चलें	वह	वे

2. *Imperative.* (प्रत्यक्ष विधि)

			चल्	
1.	ऊँ	एँ	चलूँ	चलें
2.	अ	ओ	चल	चलो
3.	ए	एँ	चले	चलें

N. B. Terminations of the *Contingent Future* and *Imperative* are identical except in second person singular, which is formed by simply adding अ to the root, or by use of the verbal stem only. From दे and ले second person plural forms are दो and लो and from आ and जा—आओ and जाओ. In first person singular दूँ and लूँ *

The *Imperative* denotes command, request, entreaty, prohibition and entreaty. It can only refer to a time after the command, request etc., is made by the speaker. It has another form in the second person. The verb in the Infinitive form (चलना, पढ़ना, लिखना etc.) is simply used both in Singular and Plural.

तू पढ़ना, तुम पढ़ना, तू मत जाना, तुम जाना

There is some difference in the use of the two Imperative forms. In the Imperative तू चल, the action is to immediately follow the command or request of the speaker. But in तू चलना the Imperative clearly refers to a somewhat distant future. Here the action (the act of going) is to begin necessarily in future or a relatively distant future. We may call तू चल as Direct Imperative and तू चलना as Indirect Imperative.

With honorific आ the termination इये or इयेगा is added to the root.

आप पढ़िये (पढ़् + इये) आप पढ़ियेगा ।

आप जाइये (जा + इये) आप जाइयेगा ।

The इयेगा forms are considered to be more polite than इये forms of the Imperative. इयेगा is a termination by adding गा to इये. गा indicates the sense of futurity.

आप इसे पढ़िये (please) read it.

आप इसे पढ़ियेगा You would (kindly) read it.

Mark that often no equivalent of 'please' in Hindī is used, but simply the use of honorific terminations serves the purpose.

दे and ले are changed to दी and ली and then ज् is inserted before इये or इयेगा is added.

---

* Roots दे and ले drop their ए before these terminations.

दीजिये, दीजियेगा; लीजिये, लीजियेगा ।

On this analogy we have पीजिये or पीजियेगा । कर् has two forms करिये and कीजिये, the former may be called regular and the latter irregular.

आप यह काम करिये, करियेगा ।

आप यह काम कीजिये, कीजियेगा ।

The कीजिये and कीजियेगा forms are being preferred now.

Roots ending in ई, ऊ and ओ

Some writers have used व् instead of य् in these future forms.

खाये, खावे; खायेगा, खावेगा; पाये, पावे; पायेगा, पावेगा;

पीये, पीवे; पीयेगा, पीवेगा; देये, देवे; देयेगा (देगा), देवेगा (देगा) ।

There is another form खायगा for खायेगा, जायगा for जायेगा, पायगा for पायेगा. Such forms are used in the Absolute Future, generally in poetry and some times in prose also by standard writers.

But for uniformity, the ये forms are being used by modern writers. So खाये; खायेगा, पाये, पायेगा; पीयेगा (also पियेगा) and जीयेगा (also जियेगा) देगा, लेगा should now be used.

Between पियेगा and पीयेगा, सियेगा and सीयेगा in my opinion the former forms are to be preferred.*

3. *Absolute Future* (सामान्य भविष्य)

Absolute Future is formed by simply adding गा to the *Contingent Future* terminations. Plural form of गा is गे and feminine form is गी.

---

* We have already pointed that ये in the verbs is also written as ए—पढ़ियेगा. पढ़िएगा. In the opinion of the present writer ये is better and this spelling is supported by the dialects, tradition and also on phonetic grounds. The controversy between scholars as to which form is correct is not of importance to the average reader, who may take both forms to be correct for the purpose of spelling, The जायगा, पायगा, optional forms of जायेगा, and पायेगा also lend support to जायेगा. and पायेगा spelling. जाँय, खाँय for जायें and खायें also support this view.

N. B. We may take गा as the letter to indicate futurity in Hindī, which assumes three forms गा गे and गी

Terminations		चल	
S.	P.	S.	P.
ऊँगा	एँगे	चलूँगा	चलेंगे
एगा	ओगे	चलेगा	चलोगे
एगा	एँगे	चलेगा	चलेंगे

The English 'shall' and 'will' are both translated into Hindī with गा (गे, गी) forms of the verb. The distinction in the English grammar regarding the use of 'shall' and 'will' is of no importance in Hindī.

Conjugation of ह् and थ्

Before we deal with the conjugation of verbs in tenses of the other groups, it is necessary to understand the peculiarities and special features of two roots √ह् and √थ् which are very important ह्, which seems to be derived from √अस् Sanskṛt has the sense of 'being' or 'isness'. There is another root in Hindi √'हो' which is derived from भू Sanskṛt. Much confusion has been caused by recognising हो only as a root and ignoring a separate root ह्. Guru says that होना is both स्थिति दर्शक and विकार दर्शक i. e. it has both the sense of '*isness*' and '*becoming*'. हो never strictly speaking denotes 'isness' or existence. हूँ, हैं, है, हो are forms of ह् and mean existence pure and simple. These are formed in the following manner हूँ—ह्+ऊँ, हैं—ह्+एँ, है—ह्+ऐ, हो—ह्+ओ. This हो is different from हो *'to become'* and should not be confused. मैं हूँ *I am*, वह है *He is*, तू है *Thou art*, तुम हो, *'You are* वह है *He is* and वे हैं *they are*. These conjugational forms of root ह् are not affected by change of gender and are not auxiliary or subsidiary verbs. वह लड़का है *He is a boy*, वह लड़की है *She is a girl*, मैं लड़का हूँ *I am a boy* or मैं लड़की हूँ *I am a girl*. तुम लड़के हो *You are a boy*, तुम लड़की हो *You are a girl*.

ह् seems fo be derived from अस्; अ of अस् is dropped and स् remains, which is changed to ह् in Hindī. अस् is a root according to Pāṇiñi. But Patañjali says that according to Āpisali the root was स्, So ह् may be directly derived from स् of Āpisali.

Conjugation of √ह

मैं हूँ—हम हैं
तू है—तुम हो
वह है—वे हैं

थ—It has the sense of *'was-ness'* or existence in past tense. It is probably derived from आसीत्, a past form of √अस्—in Sanskṛt or from स्था.

Conjugation of √थ्.

1. था थे
2. था थे
3. था थे

Thus it has only two forms in the masc. था and थे, the feminine form in sing. is थी and in plur. थीं. This थ् is influenced by gender. था means 'was' and थे means 'were' in English. थ् is also used as the main verb like ह्. But both are also used as subsidiary verbs. वह जाता है *He is going,* वह जाता था *He was going,* वह जाती है *She is going,* वह जाती थी *She was going.*

हो—Here we may deal with the conjugation of हो (होना) *become 'to happen'.* This is always used with conjugational forms of ह् (हूँ, हैं, है, हो).

हो has different forms in the present, past and future. ह् can only be used in the present and थ् in the past tense when used as main verb.

	Masc.	Fem.
Pr.	होता है	होती है
P.	हुआ था	हुई थी
F.	होगा	होगी

In the future tense हो is only used i. e. ह् as an auxiliary root does not accompany it.

Mark the following uses of होना :—

ऐसा होता है It so happens.

खेत में अनाज होता है Grains grow (literally happens) in field.

जब बच्चा होता है When a child is born (or comes out)

जब मुझे क्रोध होता है When I feel angry (I am angry) —literally when anger comes to me.

आजकल दिन छोटा होता है Days are shorter these days.

होता है has different senses in the above sentences.

होना comes after many nouns in Hindi and such combinations function as verb in Hindī.

होना also is used with the adjectival forms of several nouns in Hindī.

मोह होना—इस संसार से सबको मोह होता है ।

मोहित होना—सुन्दर रूप पर कौन मोहित नहीं होता ?

लोप होना—अंधकार होने पर तारों का लोप होता है या हो जाता है ।
Stars disappear after the darkness sets in (disappearance of stars happens after the darkness sets in)

लुप्त होना—आकाश से तारे प्रभात में लुप्त हो जाते हैं ।
Stars disappear in the sky in early morning.

प्रसार होना—रोज रेडियो द्वारा समाचार का प्रसार होता है ।
Broadcast of news daily is done by Radio.

प्रसारित होना—रेडियो द्वारा रोज समाचार प्रसारित होता है ।
News is broadcast daily by radio.

Thus होता is a separate verb, which is used in various ways in Hindī. It has no relation with ह् which has only the sense of 'is—ness' or existence. हो is a conjugational form of ह्. Thus हो is has the sense of existence तुम कहाँ हो ? *Where are you* ? This is हो is quite different from हो, a separate root, meaning *'to become'* or *'to be'*.

We have dealt with the root हो at this place as it is some time confused with हो (second person plural of ह्).

Conjugation of हो in tenses of the First Group.

Contingent future.

मैं होऊँ	— *I may be.*	हम होवें	— *We may be.*
तू होवे	— *Thou mayst be.*	तुम होओ	— *You may be.*
वह होवे	— *He may be.*	वे होवें	— *They may be.*

Absolute future.

मैं होऊँगा	*I shall be.*	हम होवेंगे (होंगे)	*We shall be.*
तू होवेगा (होगा)	*Thou wilt be.*	तुम होओगे (होंगे)	*You will be.*
वह होवेगा (होगा)	*He will be.*	वे होवेंगे (होंगे)	*They will* be.

Imperative.

Second Person. तू हो तुम हो (होओ)

Tenses of Group II and III (12 tenses)

1st pair. **Indefinite Imperfect and Indefinite Perfect** (सामान्य संकेतार्थ और सामान्य भूत)

We have already noted that Imperfect represents an action as incomplete and perfect as complete. As Indefinite forms do not refer to any particular time, past, present or future, they are called indefinite. In these forms simply the participles ता, आ, या are added to the root e.g. आता, आया. No auxiliary is used in these two tenses. मैं आता I come, मैं आया I came.

Kellog says that the Indefinite Imperfect has no precise equivalent in English. It is generally employed as a contigent, e.g. जो तुम सच बोलते *Were you speaking the truth.*

2nd pair. **Present Imperfect and Present Perfect** (सामान्य वर्त्तमान और आसन्न भूत या पूर्ण वर्त्तमान)

Both refer to the present time. The Present of auxiliary substantive ह् is added to the participle.

Pres. Imperf. १. आता हूँ, आते हैं, २. आता है, आते हो, ३. आता है, आते हैं।
Pres. Perf. १. आया हूँ, आये हैं, २. आया है, आये हो, ३. आया है, आये हैं।

3rd pair. **Past Imperfect and Past Perfect** (अपूर्ण भूत और पूर्ण भूत)

Both refer to past. The past forms of the auxiliary substantive root था is added to the participle.

Past Imperf. 1. आता था, आते थे, 2. आता था, आते थे, 3. आता था, आते थे
Past Perf. 2. आया था, आये थे, 2. आया था, आये थे, 3. आया था, आये थे

4th pair. **Contingent Imperfect and Contingent Perfect** (सम्भाव्य वर्त्तमान और सम्भाव्य भूत)

In both these tenses the action is merely a possibility.

The characteristic auxiliary is the contingent future of the substantive verbal root हो.

Conting. Imperf. 1. आता होऊँ, आते हों, होवें etc.
Conting. Perf. 2. आया होऊँ, आये हों, होवें etc.

5th pair. **Presumptive Imperfect and Presumptive Perfect** (सन्दिग्ध वर्त्तमान और सन्दिग्ध भूत)

Both represent the action as a probability.

Absolute future of हो is used as auxiliary in both the tenses.

Presump. Imperf 1. आता होऊँगा आते होंगे। etc.
Presump. Perf. 2. आया होऊँगा आये होंगे। etc.

6th pair. **Past Contingent Imperfect and Past Contingent Perfect** (अपूर्ण संकेतार्थ और पूर्ण संकेतार्थ)

Indefinite Imperfect of the substantive verbal root हो is added.

Past Conting. Imperf. 1. आता होता आते होते etc.
Past Conting. Perf. 2, आया होता आये होते etc.

Generally in these tenses जो, यदि, कदाचित्, are used to denote their contingent nature. They are used in conditional clauses implying a contingency in the past.

N. B. The last three pairs i.e. 4th, 5th and 6th pairs, are of comparatively infrequent or uncommon use.

हो-होना Verb

Tenses from Imperfect Participle ता

Indef. Imperfect.

मैं होता *I would be.*	हम होते *We would be.*
तू होता *Thou wouldst be.*	तुम होते *You would be.*
वह होता *He would be.*	वे होते *They would be.*

Present Imperfect.

मैं होता हूँ *I am becoming.*	हम होते हैं *We are becoming.*
तू होता है *Thou art becoming.*	तुम होते हो *You are becoming.*
वह होता है *He is becoming.*	वे होते हैं *They are becoming.*

N. B. The present imperfect forms are formed by adding conjugational forms of ह् (हूँ, है, हैं, हो)

Past Imperfect.

मैं होता था *I was becoming.*	हम होते थे *We were becoming.*
तू होता था *You were becoming.*	तुम होते थे *You were becoming.*
वह होता था *He was becoming.*	वे होते थे *They were becoming.*

N. B. The Past Imperfect forms are formed by adding conjugation forms of ह्.

Tenses from Perfect Participle आ

Indefinite perfect.

मैं हुआ *I become.*	हम हुए *We become.*
तू हुआ *Thou becomest.*	तुम हुए *You become.*
वह हुआ *He becomes.*	वे हुए *They become.*

Present Perfect.

मैं हुआ हूँ *I have been or become.* हम हुए हैं *We have been or become.*
तू हुआ है *Thou has been or become.* तुम हुए हो *You have been or become.*
वह हुआ है *He has been or become.* वे हुए है *They have been or become.*

Past Perfect.

मैं हुआ था *I had been or become.* हम हुए थे *We had been or become.*
तू हुआ था *Thou hadst been or become.* हम हुए थे *You had been or become.*
वह हुआ था *He had been or become.* हम हुए थे *They had been or become.*

The following five tenses of √हो are seldom used, but such constructions are often met in combination with other verbs.

1. Contingent Imperfect.
2. ,, Perfect.
3. Presumptive Imperfect.
4. ,, Perfect.
5. Past Contingent Imperfect.

Past Contingent Perfect is sometimes used.

It is difficult to give the translation of the above-noted tenses.

1. *Contingent Imperfect—*

1. मैं होता होऊँ हम होते होवें (हों)
2. तू होता होवे (हो) तुम होते होओ (हो)
3. वह होता होवे(हो) वे होते होवें (हों)

2. *Contingent Perfect—*

1. मैं हुआ होऊँ हम हुये होवें (हों)
2. तू हुआ होवे (हो) तुम हुये होओ (हो)
3. वह हुआ होवे (हो) वे हुये होवें हों)

3. *Persumptive Imperfect—*

1. मैं होता होऊँगा हम होते होंगे (होवेंगे)
2. तू होता होगा तुम होते होगे
3. वह होता होगा वे होते होंगे

4. *Presumptive Perfect*—	1. मैं हुआ होऊँगा	हम हुये होवेंगे (होंगे)
	2. तू हुआ होगा (होवेगा)	तुम हुये होगे (होओगे)
	3. वह हुआ होगा (होवेगा)	वे हुये होंगे (होवेंगे)
5. *Past Contingent Imperfect*—*	1. मैं होता होता	हम होते होते
	2. तू होता होता	तुम होते होते
	3. वह होता होता	वे होते होते
6. *Past Contingent Perfect*—	1. मैं हुआ होता	हम हुये होते
	2. तू हुआ होता	तुम हुये होते
	3. वह हुआ होता	वे हुये होते

This form if often met with यदि मैं अच्छा हुआ होता तो जरूर आता *Had I been well, I would surely have come.*

Tense Terminations

	1. Contingent. fut. mas. & fem.		2. Imperative mas. & fem.		3. Absolute fut.	
	S.	P.	S.	P.	S.	P.
1.	ऊँ	ए	ऊँ	एँ	ऊँगा (गी)	एँगे (गीं)
2.	ए	ओ	–	ओ	एगा (गी)	ओगे (गी)
3.	ए	एँ	ए	एँ	एगा (गी)	एँगे (गीं)

Verbal stem is simply used in 2nd sing. Fem-Sing गी pl. गीं

Tenses formed by terminations and conjugated forms of है and था

4. Indef. Imperf.		5. Indef. Perf.		6. Pres. Imperf.		7. Pres. Perf.		8 Past Imperf		9. Past Perf.	
S.	P.	S.	P.	S.	P.	S.	P.	S.	P.	S.	P.
ता (ती)	ते (ती)	आ, या (ई)	ए, ये (ई)	ता हूँ	ते हैं	आ, या हूँ	ए, ये, हैं	ता था	ते थे	आ, या, था	ए, ये थे
ता (ती)	ते (ती)	आ, या (ई)	ए, ये (ई)	ता है	ते हैं	अ, या है	ए, ये, हो	ता था	ते थे	आ, या, था	ए, ये,थे
ता (ती)	ते (ती)	आ, या (ई)	ए, ये (ई)	ता है	ते हैं	आ, या है	ए, ये, है	ता था	ते थे	आ, या, था	ए, ये थे

Remarks.

आ is added to a close root to make Indef. perf. य्+आ is added to an open root to make Indef. perf. पढ़्+आ=पढ़ा, आ+य्+आ=आया. ई is the fem. of आ. पी is the fem. of पा. थी is the fem. of था. थे is plur. of था, थीं is plur. of थी

Tenses formed by terminations and conjugated form of ता

10. Conting. Imf.		11. Conting. Perf.		12. Presum. Imperf.		13. Presum. Perf.		14. Past Imperf. conting.		15. Past perf. conting.	
S.	P.	S.	P.	S.	P.	S.	P.	S.	P.	S.	P.
ता होऊं	ते हों, होवें	आ, या होऊं	आ, या, हुये, हो	ता हूँगा	ते होंगे	या हूंगा	ये होंगे	ता होता	ते होते	आ, या होता	आये, होते
ता हो,	होवे ते हो, होओ	आ, हुआ हो	आ, या, हुये, हो	ता होगा	ते होगे	या होगा	ये होगे	ता होता	ते होते	आ, या होता	आये होते
ता हो,	होवे ते हों, होवें	आ हुआ हो	आ, या, हुये, हों	ता होगा	होंगे	या हूंगा	ये होंगे	ता होता	ते होते	आ, या होता	आये होते
Auxiliary-conting. future of the substantive verb.				Auxiliary Absolute future of the substantive verb.				Auxiliary Indefinite imperfect of the substantive verb.			

Remarks

Tenses from 10-15, that is, the last three pairs are of comparatively, infrequent occurrence. Of these six, except the contingent perfect, the remaining five are much less frequent.

Conjugation of root गिर् Intransitive verb गिरना to fall.

	Singular			Plural		
1. Contingent future						
I may fall etc.	1. मैं गिरूं	2. तू गिरे	3. वह गिरे	1. हम गिरे	2. तुम गिरो	3. वे गिरें
2. Absolute future						
I shall fall etc.	1. मैं गिरूंगा	2. तू गिरेगा	3. वह गिरेगा	1. हम गिरेंगे	2. तुम गिरोगे	3. वे गिरेंगे
3. Imperative						
Let me fall	1. मैं गिरूं	2. तू गिर	3. वह गिरे	1. हम गिरे	2. तुम गिरो	3. वे गिरें

Tenses of the Imperfect participle.

	Sing.			Plural		
4. Indef. Imperf.						
I would fall.	1. मैं गिरता	2. तू गिरता	3. वह गिरता	1. हम गिरते	2. तुम गिरते	3. वे गिरते
5. Pres. Imperf.						
I fall, I am falling	1. मैं गिरता हूं	2. तू गिरता है	3. वह गिरता है	1. हम गिरते हैं	2. तुम गिरते हो	3. वे गिरते हैं
6. Past Imp.						
I was falling.	1. मैं गिरता था	2. तू गिरता था	3. वह गिरताथा	1. हम गिरते थे	2. तुम गिरते थे	3. वे गिरते थे
7. Conting. Imperf.						
I may be falling.	1. मैं गिरता होऊं	2. तू गिरता हो	3. वह गिरता हो	1. हम गिरते हों	2. तुम गिरते होम्रो	3. वे गिरते हों

8. Present Imperf.						
I must be falling.	1. मैं गिरता होऊंगा	2. तू गिरता होगा	3. वह गिरता होगा	1. हम गिरते होंगे	2. तुम गिरते होगे	3. वे गिरते होंगे
9. Past Conting. Imperf.						
Were I falling.	1. मैं गिरता होता	2. तू गिरता होता	3. वह गिरता होता	1. हम गिरते होते	2. तुम गिरते होते	3. वे गिरते होते

Tenses of the Perfect participle.

	Sing.			Plural		
10. Indef. Perf.						
I fall	1. मैं गिरा	2. तू गिरा	3. वह गिरा	1. हम गिरे	2. तुम गिरे	3. वे गिरे
11. Pres. Perf.						
I have fallen.	1. मैं गिरा हूं	2. तू गिरा है	3. वह गिरा हैं	1. हम गिरे हैं	2. तुम गिरे हो	3. वे गिरे हैं
12. Past Perf.						
I had fallen.	1. मैं गिरा था	2. तू गिरा था	3. वह गिरा था	1. हम गिरे थे	2. तुम गिरे थे	3. वे गिरे थे
13. Conting. Perf.						
I might have fallen:	1. मैं गिरा होऊं	2. तू गिरा हो	3. वह गिरा हो	1. हम गिरे हों	2. तुम गिरे हो श्रो	3. वे गिरे हों
14. Presum. Perf.						
I would have fallen.	1. मैं गिरा हूंगा	2. तू गिरा होगा	3. वह गिरा होगा	1. हम गिरे होंगे	2. तुम गिरे होगे	3. वे गिरे होंगे
15. Past Conting. Perf.						
Had I fallen.	1. मैं गिरा होता	2. तू गिरा होता	3. वह गिरा होगा	1. हम गिरते होते	2. तुम गिरे होते	2. वे गिरे होते

Conjugation of Intransitive root जा to go.

Tenses of the future

	Singular			Singular		
1. Cont. fut.	1. मैं जाऊं	2. तू जाये, जावे, जाय	3. वह जाये, जावे,जाय	1. हम जायें, जावें, जांय	2. तुम जाम्रो	3. वे जाएं, जावें जांय
2. Abs. fut.	1. मैं जाऊंगा	2. तू जायेगा, जावेगा, जायगा	3. वह जायेगा, जावेगा, जाय	1. हम जायेंगे, जावेंगे, जायँगे	2. तुम जाम्रोगे	3. वे जाएँगे, जावेंगे, जायँगे
3. Imperative.	1. मैं जाऊँ	2. तू जा	3. वह जाये, जावे, जाय	1. हम जयें, जावें, जाँय	2. तुम जाम्रो	3. वे जायें, जायँ म्राप जाइये, जाइयेगा

Tenses of the Imperfect Participle

	Singular			Plural		
4. Indef. Imperf.	1. मैं जाता	2. तू जाता	3. वह जाता	1. हम जाते	2. तुम जाते	3. वे जाते
5. Pres. Impf.	1. मैं जाता हूं	2. तू जाता है	3. वह जाता है	1. हम जाते हैं	2. तुम जाते हो	3. वे जाते हैं
6. Past Impf.	1. मैं जाता था	2. तू जाता था	3. वह जाता था	1. हम जाते थे	2. तुम जाते थे	3. वे जाते थे
7. Cont. Impf.	1. मैं जाता होऊँ	2. तू जाता हो	3. वह जाता हो	1. हम जाते हों	2. तुम जाते होम्रो	3. वे जाते हों
8. Pres. Impf.	1. मैं जाता होऊंगा	2. तू जाता होगा	3. वह जाता होगा	1. हम जाते होगें	2. तुम जाते होगे	3. वे जाते होंगें
9. Past cont. Impf.	1. मैं जाता होता	2. तू जाता होता	3. वह जाता होगा			

Tenses of the Perfect Participle.

	Singular			Plural		
10. Indef. Perf.	1. मैं गया	2. तू गया	3. वह गया	1. हम गये	2. तुम गये	3. वे गये
11. Pres. Perf.	1. मैं गया हूं	2. तू जाता है	3. वह गया है	1. हम गये हैं	2. तुम गये हो	3. वे गये हैं
12. Past Perf.	1. मैं गया था	2. तू गया था	3. वह गया था	1. हम गये थे	2. तुम गये थे	3. वे गये थे
13. Cont. Perf.	1. मैं गया होऊँ	2. तू गया हो	3. वह गया हो	1. हम गये हों	2. तुम गये होश्रो	3. वे गये हों
14. Present Perf.	1. मैं गया होऊँगा	2. तू गया होगा	3. वह गया होगा	1. हम गये होंगे	2. तुम गये होगे	3. वे गये होंगे
15. Past Cont. Perf.	1. मैं गया होता	2. तू गया होता	3. वह गया होता	1. हम गये होते	2. तुम गये होते	3. वे गये होते

Conjugation of the Transitive root कर् 'to do'

	Sing.			Plur.		
1.	1. मैं करूँ	2. तू करे	3. वह करे	1. हम करें	2. तुम करौ	3. वे करें
2.	1. मैं करूँगा	2. तू करेगा	3. वह करेगा	1. हम करेंगे	2. तुम करोगे	3. वे करेंगे
3.	1. मैं करूँ	2. तू कर	3. वह करे	1. हम करें	2. तुम करो	3. वे करें
						श्राप कीजिये, कीजियेगा

Tenses of the Imp. Participle.

	Sing.			Plur.		
4.	1. मैं करता	2. तू करता	3. वह करता	1. हम करते	2. तुम करते	3. वे करते
5.	1. मैंकरता हूँ	2. तू करता है	3. वह करता है	1. हम करते हैं	2. तुम करते हो	3. वे करते हैं

6.	1. मैं करता था	2. तू करता था	3. वह करता था	1. हम करते थे	2. तुम करते थे	3. वे करते थे
7.	1. मैं करता होऊँ	2. तू करता होवे	3. वह करता होवे	1. हम करते हों	2. तुम करते होवे	3. वे करते हों
8.	1. मेंकरता होऊँगा	2. तू करता होगा	3. वह करता होगा	1. हम करते होंगे	2. तुम करते होगे	3. वे करते होंगे
9.	1. मैं करता होता	2. तू करता होता	3. वह करता होता	1. हम करते होते	2. तुम करते होते	3. वे करते होते
		Sing.			Plur.	
10.	1. मैंने किया	2. तूने किया	3. उसने किया	1. हमने किया	2. तुमने किया	3. उसने किया
11.	1, मैंने किया है	2. तूने किया हैं	3. उसने किया है	1. हमने किया है	2. उसने किया है	3. उसने किया
12.	1. मेंने किया था	2. तूने किया था	3. उसने किया था	1. हमने किया था	2. तुमने किया था	3. उसने किया हो
13.	1. मेंने किया हो	2. तूने किया हो	3. उसने किया हो	1. हमने किया हो	2. तुमने किया हो	3. उसने किया हो
14.	1. मैंने किया होगा	2. तूने किया होगा	3. उस ने किया होगा	1. हमने किया होगा	2. तुमने किया होगा	3. तुमने किया होगा
15.	1. मैंने किया होता	2. तूने किया होता	3. उसने किया होता	1. हमने किया होता	2. तुमने किया होता	3. उसने किया होता

Classification of verbs. (क्रिया के भेद)

The verb may be in Active or Passive form. The Passive form is formed by adding जाना to the Perfect Participle of the verb.

Verb.	Perfect Participle.	Passive form.
खोलना	खोला	खोला जाना
पढ़ना	पढ़ा	पढ़ा जाना
गाना	गाया	गाया जाना
सुनना	सुना	सुना जाना
कहना	कहा	कहा जाना

In many intransitive verbs we have two forms with जाना .

उठना	उठ जाना	उठाया जाना
सोना	सो जाना	सुलाया जाना
हिलना	हिल जाना	हिलाया जाना
गिरना	गिर जाना	गिराया जाना

The forms या जाना after the Perfect Participle forms of the root are really passive forms. The form with जाना added to the verbal stem is not passive — rather the construction is Active लड़का सोता है *The boy sleeps.* लड़का सो जाता है *The boy goes to sleep.* लड़का सुलाया जाता है *The boy is made to sleep.*

Remember that comparatively speaking, Passive Voice or passive construction is much less in use in Hindī.

In passive form the main verb (हिलाया, गिराया) is inflected. आ is changed to ए in Masc. plur. and ई in fem. sing. or plur.

पत्ता हिलाया जाता है	*Leaf is shaken.*
पत्ते हिलाये जाते हैं	*Leaves are shaken.*
पत्ती हिलाई जाती है	*Leaf* (small) *is shaken.*
पत्तियाँ हिलाई जाती हैं	*Leaves* (small) *are shaken.*

According to meaning and usage, Greaves has classified Hindi verbs in 8 classes :

1. Transitive.
2. Intransitive.
3. Neuter.
4. Passive—neuter.
5. Impersonal.
6. Passive.
7. Casual.
8. Compound.

1. Transitive (सकर्मक) A transitive verb is a verb which requires an object (expressed or implied) to complete its meaning , the effect of the action, denoted by the verb falls on the object.

वह रोटी खाता है—*He eats bread.* The effect of the action of eating falls on रोटी (*bread*) or the action is directed towards रोटी . So it is object here.

2. Intransitive. (अकर्मक) An Intransitive verb has no object.

There is certainly action but it is not directed towards any thing other than the subject. वह रोता है *He weeps.* The Indian grammarians say that when the object is also effected or influenced by the action of the subject (Karta or doer, the word denoting action) the verb is transitive. The subject is the door of the action, whether it is denoted by a trans. or intrans. verb. Thus in वह पुस्तक पढ़ता है *He reads a book.* 'He' is the subject.—he does 'reading' and he enjoys the fruit (फल) or the pleasure of reading. But for reading, it is necessary that there should be a book or some reading matter. But in वह रोता है *He weeps.* though he is the doer of the action of weeping, it is he only who feels the pain of weeping and no other thing is effected or influenced by the action, and so no object is necessary. There पढ़ना is a transitive and रोना an intransitive verb.

3. Passive. (कर्मवाच्य क्रिया) is active and देखा जाना is passive. When a passive verb is used, the subject is put in the Instrumental case and the object of the active verb becomes the subject. राम ने घर को देखा *Ram saw the house.* Here राम is subject, घर is object and देखा is active verb. The passive construction of the sentence will be घर राम से देखा गया Here the subject is put in the instrumental and घर becomes the subject and the passive verb agrees with घर in gender and person. Again राम ने चिट्ठी पढ़ी assumes the form चिट्ठी राम से पढ़ी गई.—The logical subject is still राम but चिट्ठी is the grammatical subject. Here the passive verb पढ़ी गई (past form of पढ़ा जाना) agrees with चिट्ठी in gender and person.

*4. *. Neuter. —A Neuter verb is also intrans. but implies a state for which the subject shows least activity or no activity.* वह सोता है *He is sleeping,* वह वहाँ पड़ा है *It is lying there.*

N.B. A verb is a word denoting some action, being or becoming. An object is a word upon which the action denoted by the verb is exerted or towards which the action is directed.

5. Passive-Neuter. Such verbs are passive and neuter at the same time. Many passive verbs have more affinity with neuter verbs.

The following illustration should be considered in this connection :—

पेड़ हिलाया जाता है — *The tree is being shaken.* Here what is said about the tree is that the tree is being shaken. It is not mentioned whether the shaking is caused by any person or thing. हिलाया जाना is a passive verb but when we say पेड़ हिलता है or पेड़ हिल जाता है the tree shakes, the simple fact is mentioned that the tree shakes. There is no reference to any cause or indication or as to whether there is a cause or not. This हिलना or हिल जाना is a passive neuter verb.

---

* The classification of neuter and passive-neuter is not dealt-with by Indian, grammarians, but it is important to understand the various forms of intransitive verbs in Hindi. It may be called अशक्त क्रिया and कर्मवाच्य अशक्त क्रिया ।

In Hindī many verbs have two forms, one active and the other passive. Thus खोलना is an active verb and खुलना is a passive neuter verb. खिड़की खोली गई *The window was opened.* There we infer that some one opened it. खिड़की खुल गई *The window opened.* Here there is no indication as to how the opening of window occurred. Again लकड़ी जलाई गई is passive, लकड़ी जल गई is neuter. In लकड़ी जलाई गयी the construction and meaning is that of a true passive verb, but in लकड़ी जल गई the form and construction is not passive. In a passive-neuter verb जाना is generally added to the verbal stem. In a passive verb, जाना is used after the form of perfect participle जाना, खुलना or खुल जाना *'to open'* is a passive neuter verb. The indifinite perfect of खुल जाना form will be खुल गया and in future it will be खुलेगा (some times खुल जायेगा also). Of फटना or फट जाना the indef. perf. will be फट गया but in future फट जायेगा or जायगा is more frequent than फटेगा The addition of जाना is generally indicative of passive. जागना is a neuter verb and जगना is a passive neuter.

Below is given a list of some verbs of which the active, passive and passive neuter forme are given :—

Active	Passive	Passive-Neuter
रोकना	रोका जाना	रुक जाना
छेदना	छेदा जाना	छिद जाना
छीनना	छीना जाना	छिन जाना
बचाना	बचाया जाना	बच जाना
काटना	काटा जाना	कट जाना
घोलना	घोला जाना	घुल जाना
बांटना	बांटा जाना	बंट जाना

Generally use of passive neuters is not always sharply distinguished from the use of passive verbs, but the passive neuter form is used, when the attention of the reader is directed to the state itself. The passive verb is used in cases in which the attention is directed to the agent also.

6. *Impersonal verb* (भाव वाच्य क्रिया) An Impersonal verb is similar to a passive verb in form. The verb assumes the form of the perfect participle and then is followed by जाना. Here the verb always remains in the form of the third person singular masculine— मुझसे यहाँ बैठा नहीं जाता, उससे चला नहीं जाता . बैठा and चला are the perf. participle forms of verbs चला and चलना। बैठ जाना and चला जाना are impersonal verbs (भावप्रधान क्रिया). The Hindī impersonal verb does not correspond with the English verb bearing that name. (खाया जाना, सुना जाना, सहा जाना are some common impersonal verbs. उससे खाया नहीं जाता, अब सहा नहीं जाता, अब मुझसे चुप नहीं रहा जाता। Mark that in such constructions and uses of the impersonal verbs, sentence is always negative and not affirmative.

7. *Causal verbs* (प्रेरणार्थक क्रिया) In English, the Causal or Causative verb, generally differs from a verb in its form. Thus the causal form of *'to eat'* is *'to feed'*. But in Hindi the verb undergoes some change in itself to give its causal form. पढ़ना-पढ़ाना, पढ़वाना In case of a large number of verbs there are two causal forms. We shall deal with the topic of causal verb separately,

8. *Compound verbs* (संयुक्त क्रिया) Two verbs combine in Hindī and this combination of verbs takes place in various ways. Illustrations of such compound verbs or combinations of verbs are गिर पड़ना, चुप बैठना, मार डालना.

The subject of compound verbs will also be dealt fully again.

Causal forms of verbs

The Causal verb is formed by adding आ or वा (व्+आ) to the stem. बनना to make, बन stem–बना (बन+अ) बनवा (बन+वा). Thus we have two forms बना and बनवा as causal roots to which ना is added to form causal verb बनाना 'to make' and बनवाना *'to cause another to make'* when a man asks or causes another man to act, the वाना forms or second causal forms are used. The आना forms (such गिराना to fell) खिलाना to feed) are actually active transitive verbs. Hindī grammarians call the आना forms as 'first causal form' and the वाना forms as 'second causal forms.'

Formation of Causal verbs

1. Add आ to the stem for the first form and वा for the second-form. Then ना is added, which in Hindī may be treated as a verb-sign.

सुनना *to hear* सुनाना *to tell* सुनवाना *to cause to tell;* पकना *to be ripe* पकाना *to cook* पकवाना *to cause to cook.*

2. The initial vowel आ, ई, ऊ, ए, ओ is shortened.

आ—जागना *to rise* जगाना *to awaken* जगवाना *to cause another to awake.*

ई—जीतना *to conquer* जिताना *to cause to conquer* जितवाना *to cause another to conquer.*

ऊ—घूमना *to go around* घुमाना *to turn around* घुमवाना *to cause another to go around.*

ए—देखना *to see* दिखाना, दिखलाना *to show* दिखवाना, दिखलवाना *to cause another to show.*

ओ—खोदना *to dig* खुदाना *to cause to dig* खुदवाना *to cause another to dig* खोदाना, खोदवाना optional forms.

N. B. ए and ओ are pronounced 'not in full.'

3. In an open root ending in ई, ऊ and ए ओ is inserted between the shortened vowel and the causal affix आ or वा.

पीना	*to drink*	पिलाना		पिलवाना
छूना	*to touch*	छुलाना		छुलवाना
देना	*to give*	दिलाना		दिलवाना
सोना	*to sleep*	सुलाना	*to put to sleep*	सुलवाना

4. The initial vowels ऐ and औ undergo no change.

दौड़ना	*to run*	दौड़ाना	दौड़वाना
तैरना	*to swim*	तैराना	तैरवाना

The second causal form (वा-form) is possible only when the first causal form denotes real activity on the part of 'doer' and not merely 'getting something done.' Thus गिराना the first causal form also denotes activity or the part of the doer, so it means *'to fell'* in English, The second causal form गिरवाना has the meaning of *'to get felled'*. Thus बनना *'to be made'* is really a Passive-neuter verb and its active form is बनाना *to make*. बनाना in form appears to be first causal of बनना but has the sense of 'to make'. बनवाना *'to cause to be made'* is the genuine causal form. Similarly पिटना *'to be beaten'* has its active form पीटना and causal form पिटवाना *to cause to be beaten*.

Below is given a list of verbs, when the first causal forms are really transitive forms, though Hindī grammarians have classified them under the first causal form. सुनाना *to tell, to relate*, उठाना *to raise* समझाना *to explain*, जगाना *to awaken*, घुमाना *to turn around*, दिखाना *to show*, सिखाना *to teach*, बुलाना *to call*, फैलाना *to spread*, खौलाना *to boil*, छुड़ाना *to liberate*, चुराना *to steal*.

Passive		Active		Causal
जलना	*to burn*	जलाना	*to burn*	जलवाना
कटना	*to be cut*	काटना	*to cut*	कटवाना
पिसना	*to be ground*	पीसना	*to grind*	पिसाना
छिदना	*to be pierced*	छेदना	*to pierce*	छिदवाना
सुनना	*to hear*	सुनाना	*to tell*	सुनवाना
समझना	*to understand*	समझाना	*to explain*	समझवाना
उठना	*to rise (of itself)*	उठाना	*to raise*	उठवाना
मिलना	*to meet*	मिलाना	*to mix*	मिलवाना
चिपकना	*to stick*	चिपकाना	*to stick*	चिपकवाना
बंधना	*to be bound*	बाँधना	*to bind*	बंधवाना
पिटना	*to be beaten*	पीटना	*to beat*	पिटवाना
हिलना	*to move*	हिलाना	*to move (tr.)*	हिलवाना
खुदना	*to be dug*	खोदना	*to dig*	खुदवाना (खोदना)
घुलना	*to be dissolved*	घोलना	*to dissolve*	घुलना (घोलवाना)
मिटना	*to be effected*	मिटाना	*to effect*	मिटवाना

Passive		Active		Causal
खिंचना	*to be drawn*	खींचाना	*to draw*	खिचवाना
फिंकना	*to be flung*	फेंकना	*to throw*	फिंकवाना (फेंकवाना)
दबना	*to be pressed*	दबाना	*to press*	दबवाना
उखड़ना	*to be uprooted*	उखाड़ना	*to uproot*	उखड़वाना
बिगड़ना	*to be spoiled*	बिगाड़ना	*to spoil*	बिगड़वाना
खुलना	*to be opened*	खोलना	*to open*	खुलवाना (खोलवाना)
बोलना	*to speak*	बुलाना	*to tell*	बुलवाना
			to cause to call. to cause another to speak	बोलवाना
बीतना	*to pass (time)*	बिताना	*to pass*	बितवाना
जोतना	*to yoke*	जुताना	*to get yoked*	जुतवाना
डूबना	*to be drowned*	डुबाना	*to drown*	डुबवाना
		डुबोना		
दौड़ना	*to run*	दौड़ाना	*to cause another to run*	दौड़वाना
फैलना	*to spread*	फैलाना	*to spread (tr.)*	फैलवाना
बैठना	*to sit*	बैठाना	*to seat*	बैठवाना
		बिठाना		बिठवाना
		बिठालना		बिठलवाना
बोना	*to sow*	बो आना	*to cause to to be sown*	
भेजना	*to send*	भेजवाना	*to cause to send*	
		भिजवाना		
		भेजाना		
डालना	*to put*	डलवाना	*to cause to put in*	
		डलाना		
मारना	*to strike*	मरवाना	*to cause to strike*	
रखना	*to keep*	रखवाना	*to cause to keep*	

Mark the causal forms of the following verbs :—

गाना *to sing* गवाना, बोना *to sow* बोआना, रोना to weep रुलाना, सीना *to stitch* सिलाना, सिलवाना, छूना *to touch* छुवाना, छुलाना, लेना to take लिवाना*

Many stems ending in ट change their ट to ड़

छूटना	*to be free*	छोड़ना	*to leave*	छुड़ाना, छुड़वाना
टूटना	*to break* or *to be broken*	तोड़ना	*to break*	तोड़वाना, तुड़वाना
फटना	*to be torn*	फाड़ना	*to tear*	फड़वाना
फूटना	*to be broken*	फोड़ना	*to break*	फोड़वाना

Some irregular formations.

बिकना	*to be sold*	बेचना	*to sell*	बेचवाना
		बिकाना	*to get sold*	बिकवाना
धुलना	*to be washed*	धोना		धुलवाना

There are some verbs, where the meaning of आना and वाना forms have little difference. Thus कराना and करवाना both are causative forms from करना but there is little difference in meaning.

मैं यह काम कराना चाहता हूं *I want this work to be done (by some one).* मैं यह काम तुमसे करवाना चाहता हूँ। *I want this work to be done by you.*

In the former sentence, I only want that the work be done, (it may be done by any body) but in the latter sentence the desire is that the work is to be done by a particular person ('you'). So causation is more pointed and the second causal form करवाना is preferred.

We have already pointed out that many आना forms are not genuine causals, rather they are active transitive verbs. There are two kinds of *kartā* ('doer') or subject, one is the actual subject and

*Some of the casual torms in Hindī cannot be properly translated into English. A literal translation will be very crude in English and so has not been attempted.

the other may be only an agent or an 'intermediary' doer. This kind of *Kartā* is not independent, but is moved or impelled by another and is an intermediary Kartā.

मोहन मकान बनाता है	*Mohan builds a house.*
मोहन मकान बनवाता है	*Mohan gets a house built,* *or Mohan causes a house to be built* (surely with the help of labourers.)

But मोहन मकान बनाता है also means that he works as a labourer in building (or constructing) the house. In Hindī grammars, we find बनना, बनाना, बनवाना forms and the two forms बनाना and बनवाना as causative forms, but we see that बनाना is in no sense causative.

This आना is also used with many nouns or adjectives. Many nouns thus become verbs and they are called Nāmadhātus.

दुख-दुखाना	*to cause pain.*
पीर-पिराना	,,
शर्म-शर्माना	*to feel shy.*
लाज-लजाना	,,
गर्म-गर्माना	*to become hot or to heat.*
ठंड-ठंडाना	*to become cold or to cool.*

In Hindī intransitive and transitive forms of a verb seem to be ordinarily etymologically connected. See कटना and काटना, बँधना and बाँधना and टूटना and तोड़ना. The intransitive forms seem to be derived from कट्, बध्, त्रुट् Sanskṛt.

Many verbs, not of Sanskṛt origin, also undergo internal vowel change in forming transitive forms from their intransitive forms. There are certain rules which are observed in forming transitive from intransitive verbs.

Formation of transitive from intransitive verbs.

In two-letter stems the initial vowel is lengthened. कट—कटना—काटना, बँध—बाँधना, पिट—पिटना—पीटना but initial इ and उ changed to its guṇa form ए and ओ, खुल—खुलना—खोलना, घिर—घिरना—घेरना, मुड़—मुड़ना—मोड़ना

Exception :—पिट—पिटना—पीटना (the reason probably is that पेटना will create confusion.)

In stems ending in ट, ट is changed to ड़ and the initial vowel is changed to its guṇa form.

फट-फटना	फाड़ना,	फूट-फूटना	फोड़ना
छूट-छूटना	छोड़ना,	टूट-टूटना	तोड़ना

Combination of Verbs. (संयुक्त क्रियायें)

Compound verbs are very common in Hindī. Strictly speaking the combination is not of two verbs, but there is combination of a conjunctive participle, a verbal noun or a substantive with a verb.

उठ जाना, खा सकना, रो पड़ना, जल उठना, सुला देना

In all these compound verbs, the first word is a verbal stem and the second word is a verb.

In आने देना, रोने लगना, जलने लगना, the combination is with the inflected form of the infinitive form.

In मेहनत करना *to labour* भोजन करना *to eat* विनती करना *to pray* the first part is a noun and the second part is a verb.

An adjective may also combine with a verb.

अच्छा लगना, बुरा लगना, भला करना ।

An adverb may also combine with a verb in some cases.

पीछे करना	*to put behind.*
पीछा करना	*to follow.*
नीचे उतरना	*to climb down.*

Kellog has noted the following varieties of such combinations with verbs and classed them under five classes.

Class I. —1. Intensives. 2. Potentials and 3. Completives—All formed with the conjunctive participle (or verbal stem)

Class II. —1. Frequentatives 2. Desideratives — All formed with verbal nouns in ए

Class III. —1. Inceptives 2. Permissives 3. Acquisitives — All formed with the infinitive.

Class IV. —1. Continuatives 2. Progressives 3. Staticals.

4. Reiteratives. — formed with imperf. and perf. participles.

Class V. —1. Nominals—formed with Substantives and Adjectives.

Class I.

A verb combines with a verbal stem (which may be treated as the conjunctive participle.)

बना देना, काट डालना, गिर पड़ना, खा जाना, पी लेना, रो बैठना, कर दिखाना, बोल उठना, सौंप रखना ।

The verbs which come after the stems to form the intensives are उठना, बैठना, पड़ना, रहना, डालना (close verbs) and आना, जाना देना, लेना (open verbs).

According to Kellog, the following idea is expressed approximately by these secondary verbs in English :

1. उठना *suddenness.*	4. रहना *continuance.*	7. जाना *finality, completeness.*
2. बैठना *permanence*	5. डालना *violence*	8. देना *intensity*
3. पड़ना *chance.*	6. आना *reflexion.*	9. लेना *reflexion, appropriation.*

देना, डालना— may be used only with a trans. verb. Exception चल देना

आना, उठना — may be used only with an intrans. verb.

बैठना, पड़ना, रहना, जाना, लेना—These may be used either with a trans. or an intrans. verb.

देना— It generally combines with causative roots.

समझा देना, बता देना ।

जाना — Generally जाना is combined with intrans. or passive verbal stems. मिल जाना, पहुँच जाना, मर जाना ।

जाना— with trans. stems.

खा जाना, कह जाना etc.

It is combined also with passive neuter verbs. आना— Sometimes आना and जाना are both used as intensives. In case of आना the action of the verb is regarded as directed towards or near the speaker. There is a slight difference in meaning of the following sentences : पेड़ की डालियाँ झुक आई हैं, झुक गई हैं । आम लटक आये हैं, आम लटक गये हैं ।

रहना— Combination of a stem with रहना is very common. It is commonly used to form the present or past perfect tense.

वह सुन रहा है। वह सुन रहा था।

Many grammarians hold the view that present and past perf. forms of the combination of रहना give rise to two tenses तात्कालिक वर्त्तमान (similar to present continuous in English).

1. वह जा रहा है। *He is going.*

2. वह जाता है। *He goes.*

3. वह जा रहा था। *He was going.*

4. वह जाता था। *He was going.*

Though both the third and fourth sentences in Hindī will be translated in English as 'He was going', in Hindī there is slightly more emphasis on the continuity of action in the third form than the fourth. It has रहना which, when a secondary verb, intensifies the sense of continuity.

लेना-देना— They convey approximately the idea of 'taking' and 'giving out' in English. There is a difference in the use of लेना and देना with the same root बुला लेना and बुला देना, उस लड़के को बुला लो *call that boy*. (there is an implication that the boy is to be called at the place where the speaker is उस लड़के को बुला दो *Call that boy*, इस किताब को रख लो *Keep this book* (with yourself is implied.)

इस किताब को रख दो — *Keep this book.*

Kellog draws the distinction between लेना and देना in this manner. लेना represents the action of the verb as terminating with upon, near or to the advantage of the agent and देना emphasises the action as terminating upon or to the advantage of one's self.

पड़ना — *'to lie, to happen, to fall.'* — It is not combined with causal roots. It combines with trans. and intrans. roots. वह रो पड़ा। *He happened to weep.* देख पड़ना *to come into view,* गिर पड़ना *to fall down.*

पड़ना— also combines with an intrans. root with आई suffix. दिखाई पड़ना, सुनाई पड़ना दिख्+आई=दिखाई, सुन+आई=सुनाई। वह मुझे रास्ते में दिखाई पड़ा — *I happened to see him on the road.*

It also comes after the negative particle नहीं between the root and the secondary verb. मुझे कुछ सुनाई नहीं पड़ता — *I cannot hear anything.*

डालना— *'to throw', 'to fling'* — It is combined with roots with which the idea of throwing or addition of force is appropriate.

काट डालना— *to cut.* दे डालना — *to give away.* तोड़ डालना— *to smash.*

उठना— *'to rise up'* with the idea of suddenness.

चिल्ला उठना — *to cry out.* वह चिल्ला उठा — *He cried out.*

बोल उठना — *to speak up.* ज्योंही मैं बोलने उठा — *As I rose to speak up.*

धधक उठना — *to blaze out.* आग धधक उठी — *The fire blazed.*

बैठना — It suggests the idea of settling down to something. चुप बैठना — वह चुप बैठा है *He is sitting (down) quietly.*

पूछ बैठा— मैं उससे पूछ बैठा — *I 'set' to ask him.*

बन बैठा — *happened to become, became.*

अंग्रेज व्यापारी बनकर आये थे और अधिकारी बन बैठे— *The English (people) came as traders and eventually became administrators*

रखना — रोक रखना — (literally to keep in a stopped position)

मैं तुम्हें रोक रखना चाहता हूँ — *I want to keep you detained (or not to allow you to move)*

समझ रखना — *to understand.* तुमने मुझे क्या समझ रखा है—*What do you think of me ?*

निकलना— *'to go out'* — जा निकलना — मैं एक ऐसी गली में जा निकला—*I came to arrive in such a lane.*

Combination with चढ़ *as the first member.*

चढ़ आना, चढ़ बैठना, चढ़ दौड़ना—

In all these cases a verb of motion comes as the second member. Perhaps the second member is not secondary in meaning. According to Kellog चढ़ adds the idea of hostility. These combinations are really speaking idioms and are so used. चढ़ आना, चढ़ाई करना—*to attack.* There seems to be the idea of strong grip also with the idea of attack. चढ़ दौड़ना, मैं उस पर चढ़ दौड़ा — *I rushingly made an attack on that.*

Many verb combinations in Hindī serve the purpose of idioms and acquire a special meaning.

Class II

Combination formed with the first part put in perf. participle form.

These may be considered under the following heads :—

1. *Frequentatives* (अभ्यासबोधक) It is combined with the perf. participle form of the first verb. Such compound verbs denote habitual or repeated performance of the action expressed by the first member.

मैं तुम्हारी शिकायत सुना करता हूँ - (सुना Perf. past सुन्)

वह मेरे घर पर आया करता है — (आया ,, ,, आ)

2. *Desideratives.* (इच्छाबोधक) चाहना It is also formed like frequentatives. चाहना is used in two different senses.

वह बोलना चाहा — *He desired to speak.*

दस बजना ही चाहता है — *It is just going to strike ten o'clock.* Here it has the sense of near future.

3. *Potentials.* (शक्तिबोधक) सकना — *'to be able'*— Its combination with the stem denotes ability to do the action expressed by the first member.

दौड़ सकना — *'to be able to run'*
मैं दौड़ सकता हूं— *I can run.*
तुम सुन सकते हो— *You can hear.*
वह दोड़ नहीं सकता— *He cannot run.*
वह सुन नहीं सकता— *He cannot hear.*

नहीं— May intervene between the two members.

सक् from शक् Sanskṛt, has the meaning of शक्ति (power) implied in it.

सकना— is conjugated in all the tenses.

4. *Completives.* (पूर्णताबोधक) चुकना — Its combination with the root denotes the completion of the act denoted by the first member.

पढ़ चुकना— मैं गोदान पढ़ चुका हूं *I have read Godan.*

मैंने गोदान पढ़ा है— means simply '*I have read Godan*...........but मैं गोदान पढ़ चुका हूँ means that *I have read and also finished or completed it.*

Sometimes चुकना has the sense of English '*already*' वह वहाँ पहुँच चुका है— *He has already reached there.* In the future, it has a meaning similar to that of future perfect in English.

जब मैं यह पुस्तक पढ़ चुकूँगा, तब तुम्हें दूँगा। *I will give this book to you when I shall have read it.*

Use of चाहिये — expresses obligation or duty. Before चाहिये an infinitive verb, inflected or uninflected is used, The verb change according to gender.

अच्छा काम करना चाहिये — masc.
बुरी बातें नहीं करनी चाहिये — fem.
तुम्हें ये ग्रन्थ पढ़ने चाहिये — plu.

चाहिये—is sometimes used with past perf. form of the stem

वह तुम्हें फँसाना चाहता है — *He wants to entrap you.*

In the past tense था is used after चाहिये।

तुम्हें जबाब न देना चाहिये था — *You ought not to have replied.*

Below is given in a tabulated form a list of secondary verbs which combine with another verbs :—

Verb.	Form in which used	Example	Remarks.
1. सकना	with verbal stem	वह पढ़ सकता है *He can read.*	सकना is conjugated as intransitive.
2. चुकना	,,	मैं खा चुका हूं। *I have eaten*	This is only used to form a compound verb.
3. लगना	with inflected infinitive.	वह कहने लगा। *He began speaking.*	It is not used alone in the sense of 'to begin', conjugation as intransitive verb.
4. देना	,,	उसे जाने दो। *Let him go.*	

Verb	Form in which used.	Example	Remarks
5. पाना	with inflected infinitive.	अभी खाने भी नहीं पाया था कि गाड़ी आ गयी । *He had not yet been able to eat when the covey-ance came.*	
6. करना	with perf. parti-ciple from the root.	वह पढ़ा करता था । वे आया करते थे । *He used to read. They used to come.*	It gives the sense of continuity, repe-tition or habit
7. रहना	with imperf. or perf. participle of the first verb and agrees with it in number and gender.	मैं पढ़ता रहता था । मैं पड़ा रहता था । *I used to read. I used to lie down.*	It denotes conti-nuity of action of first verb.
8. जाना	,,	लड़का जाता रहा । लड़की जाती रही । *The boy was going on. The girl was going on.*	* It also shows that the action is in progress.
9. चाहना	with inflected infinitive or gerund having form of perf. participle.	मैं सुनना चाहता हूँ । *I want to hear.* मकान गिरना चाहता है । *The house is to fall.*	Sometime desire or imminence is denoted.

Class III--formed with the Inflected Infinitive

Inceptives. (आरम्भ बोधक) लगना—It denotes the commencement of action of the first verb.

---

* When used as idiom it may mean the boy had died.

जब वे बोलने लगते हैं—*When he begins to speak.*
Here 'वे' is honorific.

वह मारने लगा—*He began to beat.*

Permissives. (अनुमतिबोधक) देना—It comes after the inflected infinitive form of the verb. It denotes permission in a general sense.

मुझे आने दो—*Let me come.*

उसने मुझे अपने घर में घुसने दिया—*He allowed me to enter into his house.*

मुझे कहने दो—*Allow me to speak.*

Acquisitives. (प्राप्तिबोधक) पाना—It is the converse of **देना**—It is used with the first verb or with the inflected infinitive form of the verb.

मैं भीड़ के मारे मन्दिर में घुस नहीं पाया ।

I could not enter into the temple because of crowd.

मैं शोर के मारे (या कारण) कुछ भी सुन नहीं पाया ।

I could not hear anything because of noise.

ज्योंही वह वहाँ पहुँच पाया था कि वर्षा होने लगी ।

Hardly had he reached there when rain began.

ज्योंही मैं लौटने पाया था कि जोरों का हल्ला हुआ ।

Hardly had I lied down when a wild noise began.

मैं अभी बैठने भी नहीं पाया था कि बाबूजी मुझ पर बिगड़ने लगे ।

Hardly had I taken my seat when papa began scolding me.

Class IV—Combinations formed with Imperf. and perf. participles.

Continuatives. (निरन्तरताबोधक) रहना—It combines with imperf. or perf. form of the first verb and denotes the continuance of an incomplete action.

मैं कहता रहता हूँ—*I go on talking.*

तुम सुनते रहते हो—*You keep on hearing.*

जो पढ़ा रहता है वह जल्द नहीं भूलता—*What is already read is not easily forgotten.*

Progressives (सातत्यबोधक) जाना—It denotes the action of the first verb as steadily progressing.

लड़का सड़क पर रोता जाता है—*The boy is weepingly going on the road.*

तुम लिखते जाते हो—*You go on writing.*

वह मेरे साथ रोज स्कूल चला जाता है—*He daily goes to school along with me.*

Sometimes the perf. participle takes the oblique singular form. Here the verb denotes continued progress of the action in the same condition.

पिये जा—*go on drinking.*

पिलाये जा—*go on offering drink.*

Staticals. (नित्यताबोधक)—A verb of motion is confined with an imperf. participle in the inflected masculine singular.

वह गाते हुए आता है—*While singing he is coming.*

वह गाती हुई आती है—*While singing she is coming.*

वह गाती आती है—*Here* हुई *is omitted.*

Reiteratives. (पुनरुक्त संयुक्त क्रियायें)—Two verbs of similar meaning and generally similar in sound also combine with each other.

वह बिना कुछ कहे सुने चला गया—*Without saying (informing) anything he went away.*

कहते-सुनते बहुत समय बीत गया—*Much time passed while talking.*

पुरखों की सारी कमाई फूँक-फाँक कर वह संन्यासी हो गया—*After squandering all ancestral earnings he became an ascetic.*

सोच-साचकर काम करना चाहिये—*One should act after fully thinking (or pondering) over it.*

In such words फूँक-फाँक, सोच-सांचकर etc. (latter members of the compound such as फाँक and साच are not independently used.)

Class V. Nominals

(नामबोधक क्रियायें) combination with substantives or adjectives.

A noun or an adjective is combined with a verb to denote one general conception. Such compound verbs are generally formed with the help of करना and होना e g. खड़ा करना *to stand* (trans.) खड़ा होना *to stand* (intrans.)

होना gives a passive sense to the verb in many cases. Thus प्राप्त करना (पाना) '*to obtain*' but प्राप्त होना (मिलना) '*to be obtained.*'

In modern Hindī, the tendency to use compound verbs, formed by Sanskṛt substantives with करना या होना, in place of common Tadbhava is growing. It should be checked, otherwise Hindī style would lose much of its freshness and vigour. Authors are using such Sanskṛt and Hindī compound verbs, thereby making the style pedantic and elegant. We may in many cases use simpler Hindī verbs in their place.

पालन करना, परिपालन, } पालना	*to protect*	अभ्यास करना	*to practise*
		अनुमान करना	*to suppose*
त्याग करना, त्यागना, परित्याग करना } छोड़ना	*to give up*	अपमान करना	*to insult*
		चेष्टा करना	*to strive*
		न्याय करना	*to judge*
भोजन करना - खाना	*to eat*	मोह करना	*to infatuate*
भंग करना, तोड़ना	*to break*	प्रेम करना	*to love*
भोग करना, भोगना	*to enjoy*	दया करना	*to pity*
आच्छादन करना-ढकना	*to cover*	श्रवण करना, सुनना	*to hear*
		मनन करना	*to think*
दहन करना, जलाना	*to burn*	कथन करना, कहना	*to tell*
निवारण करना, हटाना, दूर करना	*to remove*	विरोध करना	*to oppose*
रोकना	*to prevent*		
बध करना, हत्या करना } मार डालना	*to murder* *to kill*	चिन्ता करना	*to think* *to be anxious*
		आनन्द करना	*to enjoy*
सहन करना-सहना	*to bear*	मुग्ध करना	*to infatuate*
अध्ययन करना-पढ़ना	*to read*	शासन करना	*to govern*
इच्छा करना, अभिलाषा करना } चाहना	*to desire*	विद्रोह करना	*to rebel*
		प्रतिवाद करना	*to protest*

पूजा करना, पूजना	*to worship*	खोज करना	*to search*
परीक्षा करना, परखना	*to test*	शुद्ध करना	*to purify*
		प्रस्थान करना	*to go, to start*
संचय करना, जोड़ना, जुटाना	*to join*	स्वागत करना	*to welcome*
		क्रय करना, खरीदना	*to purchase*
विचार करना, विचारना, सोचना	*to think*	आग्रह करना	*to insist*
		आकर्षण करना, खींचना	*to attract*
स्वीकार करना, अंगीकार करना, मानना, मान लेना	*to agree*, *to accept*	अनुरोध करना	*to request*
		विनय करना	*to pray*
प्रणाम करना, नमस्कार करना	*to salute*	अनुनय करना	
विदा करना	*to bid farewell*	कल्याण करना, मंगल करना	*to do some good act*

However, the compound verbs formed from Sanskṛt substantives and their simpler forms commonly used do not have the same sense.

मैं भाई को देखने आया हूँ	*I have come to see my brother.*
भगवान का दर्शन करने मंदिर में जाना है।	*I have to go to temple with a view to see God.*

It would be intolerable in Hindī if देखने is used for दर्शन करने here. The Sanskṛt verbs are considered as more dignified and elegant.

1. दर्शन करना, देखना — *to see*
2. पदार्पण करना, आना — *to come*
3. प्रस्थान करना, जाना — *to go.*
4. भोजन करना, खाना — *to eat.*
   ग्रहण करना *to accept.* लेना *to take.*
5. परीक्षा करना *to examine.* परखना *to test.*

There is difference in meaning in compound verbs formed with a Sanskṛt substantive and a verb formed by simply adding ना to the substantive.

Ex. भोगकरना and भोगना

मोह करना and मोहना

भोग करना *to enjoy* (earthly pleasure)

भोगना *to experience pleasure or pain both.*

वह बड़ा कष्ट भोगता है *He is experiencing great pain or trouble.*

वह सुख भोगता है—*He is experiencing great pleasure.*

Many verbs like खाना, देना, लेना, मारना, आनना, मानना, चलाना, देखना, धरना, पकड़ना are used with nouns with Sanskṛt and non-Sanskṛt substantives and then they convey a special sense or are used as idioms.

A list of such compound verbs is given below :—

खाना—हवा खाना, जूता खाना, गम खाना, टक्कर खाना, धोखा खाना, रूप-खाना, मार खाना, शपथ(कसम)खाना, मूर्छा खाना ।

देना—उधार देना, ऋण (कर्ज) देना, कष्ट देना, क्लेश देना, दुःख देना, दुहाई देना, ललकार देना, पुकार देना ।

मारना—झपट्टा मारना, ठट्ठा मारना, डुबकी मारना, डींग मारना, चिंघाड़ मारना, मुक्का मारना, मुक्की मारना, चुग्गे मारना, गप्प मारना, लात मारना, हाथ मारना, शेखी मारना ।

आना—याद आना, हाथ आना, काम आना, खेत आना ।

चलाना—मुँह चलाना, बात चलाना, काम चलाना, चर्चा चलाना, देह चलाना ।

धरना—ध्यान धरना, कान धरना, नाम धरना ।

मानना—खेद मानना, दुख मानना, शोक मानना, हार मानना, बुरा मानना, भला मानना, एहसान मानना, धाक मानना, कहा मानना, बात मानना ।

लेना—दम लेना, मोल लेना, उधार लेना, विदा लेना, साँस लेना, जान लेना, आहट लेना, अंदाज लेना, पता लेना, काम लेना ।

लगाना—दाँव लगाना, दोष लगाना, पता लगाना, मुँह लगाना ।

होना--लोप होना, अन्तर्धान होना, विदा होना, प्रकाश होना, गायक होना, गुम होना, गुमसुम होना, चुप होना ।

रखना--ध्यान रखना, बीच रखना, प्रेम रखना, सुध रखना, याद रखना ।

बनाना--काम बनाना, दाम बनाना, उल्लू बनाना, बेवकूफ बनाना ।

Use of कर, के or करके with the stem.

Expressions like खाकर or खा के (having eaten) जाकर, जाके, जा करके (having gone) सुनकर, सुनके, सुनकर के are often met in Hindī. Out of these three forms the first forms with कर (like खाकर, जाकर, सुनकर are preferred by modern writers. In colloquial speech however जाके, खाके, सुनके are often used. जा करके, खा करके, सुन करके are discarded these days and are not considered elegant.

But sometimes the conjunctive participle कर, के are omitted and the stem only serves the purpose.

यह सुन मेरा मन बेचैन हो गया—*Having heard it, my mind became worried.* Here कर or के is omitted.

In poetry this कर or के is often omitted.

N. B. करके is used to intensify the meaning but there is a growing tendency to discard its use.

वह दौड़ करके आया है—*He has come running,* करके has also the sense of 'by' तुम बिगड़ करके मेरा कर क्या लोगे ? *What can you do to me by being sore with me ?* तुम बिगड़ करके मेरा क्या कर लोगे ? also has the same meaning. Only करके intensifies the meaning.

After कर only के is used. कर after कर (main verb) does not sound well, so only के is used.

यह काम करके तुम जा सकते हो *You may go after doing this work or having done this work.*

Noun of Agency (कर्तृवाचक संज्ञा)

The noun of Agency is formed by adding वाला to an inflected verb.

The inflected form of an infinite verb is formed by changing the final आ into ए. Ex. जाना-जाने-जानेवाला, खाना-खाने-खानेवाला, सोना-सोने-सोनेवाला, पढ़ना-पढ़ने-पढ़नेवाला Noun of Agency.

Fem. of खानेवाला, will be खानेवाली and mas. plu. will be खानेवाले. Similarly जानेवाली, सोनेवाली, पढ़नेवाली and जानेवाले, सोनेवाले, पढ़नेवाले etc.

Use of Adverbial Participle ही

ही is added to the oblique form of the Imperfect Participle and has the sense of 'immediately' 'or' 'as soon as'

Stem	Imperf. Participle	Oblique form
जा	जाता	जाते ही
खा	खाता	खाते ही
सो	सोता	सोते ही

This ही is added to the oblique form of the perf. participle also—खाया-खाये ही, लेटा-लेटे ही । वह बिना खाये ही चला गया—*He went away without taking food.* वह लेटे ही लेटे बोला—*He spoke while lying down.*

Quite a large number of verbs in Hindī are 'onomatopoetic' according to Greaves. The stem of such verbs ends in आ. They are, formed by duplicating the first part of the verb and then adding the usual ना. Ex. सनसना-ना. झनझना-ना, थरथरा-ना, कड़कड़ा-ना खटखटा-ना, टिपटिपा-ना, गड़गड़ा-ना etc. सनसनाना is सन+सन+आ+ना, झनझनाना झन+झन+आ+ना and so on.

Some important features of Hindī verb

1. The infinitive form of the verbs has ना at the end, as पढ़ना, लिखना. This ना is added to verbal stem, as पढ़, लिख, रो, बो etc. In a root ending in consonant, like लिख्, पढ्, सुन् चल् अ is added to the root. Thus लिख् is root and लिख (लिख्+अ) is stem.

2. This infinitive form पढ़ना or लिखना is strictly speaking a verbal noun, denoting the action or state signified by the verb. Its derivation from पठनं or लिखनं (Sanskṛt) also indicates that it is a verbal noun in meaning. The oblique form of the verb is formed by changing the final आ to ए — पढ़ना=पढ़न्+आ—पढ़न्+ए=पढना. पढ़ने, लिखने, सुनने, कहने are oblique forms of पढ़ना, लिखना, सुनना and कहना।

3. There are three kinds of participles — Imperfect, Perfect and Conjunctive. From पढ़—पढ़ता is imperf. and पढ़ा is perf. participle form. पढ़ कर or पढ़के is the form by adding conjunctive

participle कर or के. Both imperf. and perf. participles are affected by gender and number of the noun they qualify.

बहता जल निर्मल होता है	*Flowing water is clean.*
बहती धारा सुन्दर लगती है	*A flowing stream looks beautiful.*
खिला फूल तोड़ लाओ	*Pluck a blossomed flower.*
खिली कली मत तोड़ो	*Don't pluck a blossomed bud.*

So imperf. and perf. participles are also called Adjectival participles.

4. A Noun of Agency is formed by adding वाला to the inflected; सोना—सोने वाला, रोना—रोने वाला, होना—होने वाला।

5. In Hindī there are 15 tenses. Except in the contingent Future and Imperative, distinction of gender is expressed. Distinction of number is made by inflection in all the tenses.

6. In the Imperative in second person sing. only the stem is used. In other tenses terminations of second and third person sing. are the same. Plural terminations of first person and third person are identical.

7. The Conjunctive Future, the Absolute Future and the Imperative are formed by simply adding terminations to the stem. Except the Indenfinite imperf. and Indefinite perf. all other tenses are formed by participles combined with an auxiliary verb.

Voice. (वाच्य)

In Hindī there is difference among grammarians about the concept of Voice (वाच्य). Some maintain that Voice is same as Construction (प्रयोग) and they follow Sanskṛt grammarians in this matter. But Guru maintains that it is difficult to define वाच्य (Voice) but simply taking into consideration the form of the verb. In Sanskṛt both प्रयोग and वाच्य are synonymous and they make no difference. In a sentence, the difference in the concept of the 'logical subject' and the 'grammatical subject,' and the 'logical object' and 'grammatical object' should be clearly understood.

If the logical subject is also the grammatical subject then the sentence is in subjectival construction, कर्तृरि प्रयोग and it is active voice, (कर्तृ वाच्य) but if the logical subject is followed by से and the logical object is in the direct case the sentence is in objectival construction (कर्मणि प्रयोग) and it is passive voice.

सीता पुस्तक पढ़ती है — *Sita reads a book.*

(कर्तृ वाच्य) Active voice— Subjectival construction.

सीतासे पुस्तक पढ़ी जाती है— *A book is read by Sita.*

(कर्म वाच्य) Passive voice — *Objectival construction.*

If the subject is neither the 'Karta' (doer) of the action denoted by the verb, nor the object, but simply action is denoted by the verb, then the voice is called भाववाच्य (impersonal voice) in Hindī. This is only with intransitive verbs. मुझसे चला नहीं जाता *I cannot go.* Literally, *going cannot be done by me.*

Both in passive (कर्मवाच्य) and inpersonal voices (भाववाच्य) the actual or logical 'Karta' is followed by से (or द्वारा)

In impersonal voice (भाववाच्य) the verb is intransitive and the construction is neutral. Here the past participle form of the main verb is combined with form of verb जाना. It may be treated as a variety of passive voice for intransitive verbs. The verb neither agrees with the subject, nor with the object, but is always masc. sing. plur. मुझसे चला नहीं जाता—'चलना' is the principal verb and is in the past participle form and जाता is a form of जाना.

Sentences in impersonal voice are generally negative.

SECTION III

ADVERB, PREPOSITION, CONJUNCTION AND INTERJECTION

CHAPTER XI

Adverb

An adverb is a word which adds to, modifies or qualifies a verb. In Hindī, it may be a pure adverb (i. e. a word qualifying a verb) or a pronominal adverb or an adverbial phrase.

वह अच्छा गाता है — *He sings well.* अच्छा qualifies गाता है (verb) मेरी बात ध्यान से सुनो *Hear my talk attentively.* Here ध्यान से is an adverbial phrase.

मैं अब घर जाऊँगा— I will go home now.

The place of an adverb may change in Hindī.

वह गाता अच्छा है। ध्यान से मेरी बात सुनो। अब मैं घर जाऊँगा।

Adverbs can be grouped into three classes :—

1. Adverbs formed from pronouns.
2. Adverbs formed otherwise.
3. Adverbial phrases.

Adverbs formed from pronouns

Many adverbs are formed from यह, वह, जो, सो and कौन These pronouns have their bases as य, व, ज, त and क which in their oblique forms become इ, उ, जि, ति, कि (इस, उस, जिस, तिस, किस) respectively. An adverb may denote time, place, direction or manner.

All pronominal adverbs are given below in a tabulated form with their bases in the nominative and oblique forms. It would help the reader in understanding the structure and formation of such adverbs. In Hindī the following suffixes are *Adverbial suffixes* :

ब— (suffix forming adverbs of time) अब, जब, तब, कब।

हाँ— (suffix forming adverbs of place) यहाँ, जहाँ, तहाँ, कहाँ ।[1]

धर— (suffix forming adverbs of direction) इधर, जिधर, तिधर, किधर ।

यों— (suffix forming adverbs of manner) यों, ज्यों, त्यों, क्यों ।

Pronoun. यह	वह	जो	सो	कौन	form after adding emphatic ही
Nom. base. य	व	ज	त	क	
Obl. base. इ	उ	जि	ति	कि	
Time Prox. Dem. अब *Now*	Rem. Dem.	Rela-tive. जब *when*	Co-re-lative तब *then*	Inter-ogation कब *when*	अब+ही=अभी जब+ ही=जभी तभी, कभी
Place यहाँ	वहाँ	जहाँ	तहाँ	कहाँ	यहाँ+ही=यहीं वहीं, जहीं, तहीं, कहीं
Direction. इधर Hither	उधर thither	जिधर Whi-ther.	तिधर Thi-ther.	किधर Whi-ther.	
Manner. यों Thus		ज्यों as	त्यों so	क्यों why	

The above-noted adverbs of time, place and direction are also followed by से and का *vibhaktis* (case - signs) and then again convey the adverbial idea.

से—अबसे *hence forth.* यहाँ से *from here,* इधर से *from this side.* का—अब का *of this time* यहाँ का *of this place* इधर का *of this side.*

(1) तहाँ and तिधर are used in dialects. They are not independently used in standard Hindī. They are however used as co-relative adverbs with जहाँ and जिधर, as जहाँ-तहाँ, जिधर-तिधर ।

* As there is already ह at the end of यहाँ, वहाँ etc, ई only of हीं is added.

Many of the above-noted adverbs are combined with तक or तलक (upto) to give explicit adverbial meaning. अब तक Until now, तब तक 'uptill then or until then', अब तलक *uptill now*, कब तलक *how long* जहाँ तक *as far as*, कहाँ तक *how far* यहाँ तक *thus far* वहाँ तलक *so far there* इधर तक *upto this side.*

The following peculiarities about adverbs in Hindī should be noted :

1. Repetition of the pronominal adverbs—जब-जब, जहाँ-जहाँ कभी-कभी *sometimes, occasionally.*

2. Sometimes two co-relative adverbs are used together. अब तब now and then यहाँ-वहाँ here and there जहाँ तहाँ here and there इधर-उधर hither and thither जब कभी whenever जहाँ कहीं wherever.

3. 'न' between two adverbs expresses indefiniteness, कहीं न कहीं *some-where* जब न तब *at some time* कभी न कभी *sometime or other.*

4. का—intervenes between a relative and correlative adverb; ज्यों का त्यों *in the same form as it is,* जहाँ का तहाँ *at the same place where it was.*

Some peculiarities about the use of these pronominal adverbs

अब—In narration, it is often used like the English 'now' अब मैं पछताने लगा *Now I began to repent.* Here अब means 'after that'

अभी—It means *'just now'*. In a sentence it is used sometimes with कि, which introduces a new clause अभी मैं वहाँ पहुँचा भी नहीं था कि पानी बरसने लगा–*I had not even reached there that the rains came.*

अभी-अभी—To give an emphatic force on 'just now' अभी is repeated.

कभी—*'sometime'* कभी-कभी *at sometimes,* occasionally. कभी नहीं *never.* कभी न कभी *at sometimes or other* जब कभी *whereever.*

कहीं—*Somewhere* कहीं-कहीं *'at some places'.* कहीं जहाँ *whenever* कहीं न कहीं *somewhere,* सब कहीं *everywhere.*

कहीं का—वह कहींका माल उड़ा लाया है—*He has brought something from some place* (which is unknown).

वह कहीं का बदमाश है—*He is a very bad man or a great rascal.*

कहीं—*perhaps, probably, by chance* कहीं तुम समय पर न आये तो मैं बड़ी परेशानी में पड़ जाऊँगा *Perchance you won't come in time, I will be put in great difficulty.*

वह मुझसे कहीं होशियार है—*He is far more intelligent than I.*

ज्यों—ज्यों ज्यों *in proportion to,* ज्यों-ज्यों वह उम्र में बढ़ता था, उसका सौन्दर्य भी त्यों-त्यों बढ़ता जाता था *As he was growing in age, so his beauty was also growing (that is, in the same proportion).*

ज्यों ही—*as soon as,* ज्यों का त्यों—*just in the same form,* यों—*in this manner,* योंही—*without any specific purpose.*

मैं योंही यहाँ चला आया—*Just by the way, I came here.*

यों मैं कुछ नहीं कह सकता—*I can't say any thing off hand.*

यों तो वह अच्छा आदमी है—*He is a good man by the way.*

क्यों कर—*How,* this is often used in colloquial for कैसे

क्यों कर मैं यहाँ आया, यह तुम्हें कैसे बताऊँ ? *How am I to describe to you how* (or *in what manner*) *I came here.*

ज्यों-त्यों—is correlated to त्यों-त्यों, which is often un-expressed.

ज्यों-ज्यों बात बढ़ने लगी, त्यों त्यों दोनों का क्रोध बढ़ने लगा—*As the talks developed, so their anger also grew.*

इधर-उधर—*Hither and thither* इधर-उधर मत घूमो —*don't roam hither and thither;* जिधर-तिधर—*this way, that way.*

पुलिस को देखकर भीड़ जिधर-तिधर हटने लगी—*The crowd began to disperse hither and thither at the sight of the Police.*

जैसे-तैसे—*any way; any how.*

मैं वहाँ से जैसे-तैसे भाग निकला—*anyhow I fled from there.* ऐसा-वैसा *of this kind or that kind.*

मुझे उसका काम ऐसा अच्छा लगता है कि क्या कहूँ—*How much I like his work, I can't say.*

जो वैसा सोता है, वह काम क्या करेगा ?—*One who sleeps like that what work may he do ?*

ऐसे, वैसे, कैसे, जैसे, तैसे—that is, oblique forms of ऐसा, वैसा, कैसा, जैसा and तैसा are also used as *adverbs of manner.*

ऐसे—*in this manner* ऐसे यह मत करो *Don't do it in this manner.*

वैसे—*in that manner* वैसे क्यों बोलते हो ? *why do you speak that way or in that manner ?*

कैसे— *In what manner* कैसे तुम वहाँ जाओगे ?—*In what manner will you go there ?*

जैसे-तैसे—*in any manner.* जैसे तैसे मैं काम समाप्त कर भागा। *Anyhow (or in any manner) after finishing the work, I ran away.*

कुछ—बुखार कुछ कम हो गया है—*The fever has come down a little.*

बहुत कुछ—*a great deal.* वह अब बहुत कुछ अच्छा हो गया है। *He has recovered a great deal (or to a great extent).*

इतने में—*in the meanwhile.* मैं उससे बातें कर रहा था कि इतने में हेड मास्टर चले आये *I was talking to him, in the meanwhile the headmaster came.*

आप से आप—*Spontaneously or involuntarily.* वह आप से आप चल पड़ा *He spontaneously went away.*

जहाँ का तहाँ—मैं सब कुछ जहाँ का तहाँ छोड़ कर चला आया *I came leaving every thing, at the very place where it was or remained.*

Adverbs are divided into four groups

1. Adverbs of time. (कालवाचक) बाद *after.* हमेशा *always* फिर *again.*

2. Adverbs of place (स्थानवाचक) and direction (दिशावाचक) आगे *in front* पीछे *behind* नीचे *below* ऊपर *above* बाँयें *left.*

3. Adverbs of manner (रीतिवाचक) अचानक *suddenly.* धीरे-धीरे *slowly.* सचमुच *truly.* अवश्य *necessarily.*

4. Adverbs of degree (परिमाणवाचक) लगभग *almost* बिलकुल *carefully* बहुत *much* कम *little* केवल *only* अत्यन्त *exceedingly* निरा *entirely* कुछ *somewhat* बड़ा *very.*

Adjectives used as adverbs

'बहुत'—*very.* वह बहुत अच्छा लिखता है — *He writes very well.*

In English an adjective which comes before another adverb is also considered to be an adverb. Really speaking here the first adjective बहुत intensifies the sense of अच्छा which qualifies लिखना.

Note that according to English grammarians an adverb qualifies any part of speech, except a noun or a pronoun (Nesfield).

अच्छा— केला मुझे अच्छा लगता है। *I like plantain.*

Here अच्छा is really an adjective but here it is an adverb qualifying लगना.

Noun used as adverb

Many nouns are used as adverbs, when used with case-signs को, से, में, पर।

रात को मैं आऊँगा —	*I will come at night.*
शाम से पानी बरस रहा है —	*It is raining since (last) evening.*
देरसे बाजारसे मत लौटना।	*Do not return late from the market.*

At some places the case-signs are omitted. Still the word carries adverbial sense. Such nouns often come after numerals or pronominal forms.

किस समय तुम आवोगे ?	At what time will you come ?
कई दिन पहले की बात है।	It happened some days ago.
एक पल भी मैं नहीं ठहर सकता।	I can't wait even for a moment.

Adverbial phrases

When a noun or an adjective and an adverb combines with case-signs, such forms may be treated as adverbial phrases. Ex. नम्रता से *gently*, ध्यान से *attentively*, अन्त में *finally*, वास्तव में *really*. चुपके से *silently*, सहज में *easily* झट से, पल में, पलभर में *in a moment* थोड़ी देर में *in a short time etc.*

Combination of adverbs

An adverb may combine with itself or with another adverb or a noun. धीरे-धीरे *slowly*, नहीं तो *if not then*, और कहीं *elsewhere*. कभी नहीं *never* क्यों नहीं ? *why not* ?

To express the adverbial idea often के or करके is added to the conjunctive participle of a word.

जान के कोई आग में हाथ नहीं डालता — *Nobody would knowingly put his hand in fire.*

खास करके तुमसे मैं यह भेद कहता हूँ — *Mainly I tell you this secret.*

Below is given a list of important adverbs of time, place and manner in common use.

Adverbs of time :— आगे *before* आज *today* कल *yesterday or tomorrow* तड़के, भोरे *at break of day* तुरत, तुरन्त *immediately* परसों *day before yesterday or day after tomorrow.* तरसों *three days ago or three days hence* पीछे *after-wards, after* फिर, पुनः *again* नित्य-नित्य *daily, constantly,* बारबार, बारम्बार *repeatedly,* अन्त में *at last* सदा, सर्वदा, हमेशा *always* पहले *previously* पीछे *subsequently* इतने में *meanwhile* अक्सर, प्रायः *often.*

Adverbs of place :— पार *across* पास *near* आस-पास *on both or all sides, near to it* आर-पार *on both sides* (of a river or sea), बाहर *outside, without,* भीतर *inside, within,* आगे *ahead* पीछे *behind.* Sanskṛt अन्यत्र *elsewhere,* एकत्र *at one place* सर्वत्र *everywhere* अत्र *here* तत्र *there* निकट *near* etc.

Adverbs of manner :— अचानक *Suddenly,* जानो *so to speak* मानो *as if* झटपट *very quickly,* ठीक *exact, correct,* ठीक *exactly,* धीरे *slowly* पैदल *on foot* बहुत *very, much,* लगातार *incessantly,* सच *truly,* सचमुच *truly* सेंत में *gratis* सेंतमेंत *gratis, without any price,* हौले *slowly* एकाएक *suddenly* एकबारगी *all at one time* धड़ाधड़ *boldly, without break,* मनमाने *according to one's will or desire,* Sanskṛt अकस्मात् *suddenly* अति, अतिशय, अत्यंत *very, very much,* अधिक *much,* अर्थात् *that is* केवल, मात्र *only, merely* निरन्तर, *incessantly, continuously* परस्पर *mutually,* यथा *as* अनायास *easily,* तथा *so,* वृथा *in vain,* शीघ्र *quickly,* सहज *naturally,* स्वभावतः *naturally, by nature,* सहसा *unexpectedly,* सत्य *truly,* स्यात् *perhaps,* सारांशतः *summarily,* संक्षेपतः *in brief,* सर्वथा *in every way,* अन्यथा *in another manner,* विधिवश *luckily,* कृपया *kindly,* विशेषतः *specially,* कदाचित् *probably,* किंचित् *some,* वस्तुतः *really,* क्रमशः *in some order,* पूर्ववत् *as previously,* परस्पर *traditionally.*

Urdu adverbs

जल्द, जल्दी—*quickly,* शायद *perhaps,* अलबत्ता *certainly, indeed,*

खासकर *specially*, सिर्फ़, फ़क़त *only*, बिलकुल *altogether*, याने *that is to say*, फ़ौरन *soon*.

Notes on some common adverbs

आगे-पीछे—They refer to place and time both, forward-backward.

आगे बढ़ो—move onward.

आगे की बात मैं नहीं कह सकता—*I cannot say what will happen in future.*

मेरे घर के पीछे एक गली है—*There is a lane behind my house.*

अभी तुम यह नहीं समझ रहे हो, पीछे तुम्हें स्वयं अनुभव होगा। *You do not understand now but would yourself experience it afterwards.*

कभी—It denotes indefinite tense.

कहाँ—कहाँ आप और कहाँ मैं? *What a difference between you and me.* At such places **कहाँ** denotes great difference.

कहीं—At some places it has the sense of perhaps or possibly.

कहीं किसी ने मालिक से आकर कह दिया तो—*If somebody comes and speaks to the master.*

परे—It conveys the idea of **दूर**

परे हट—*get away*

योंही—तुम योंही क्यों घूमा करते हो? *Why you wander aimlessly ?*

कबका—*from a long time.*

कबका मैं यहाँ खड़ा हूँ—*From a long time, I am standing here.*

न—In interrogative sentences, it has not the sense of negative.

आओगे न ? *will you come ?*

न *no*, **नहीं** *not*, **नहीं तो** *if not, otherwise*, are used sometimes in adverbial sense and called by grammarians as *Adverbs of Negation.*

हाँ—Similarly हाँ *yes,* जी *yes,* जी हाँ Yes, sir; are also used in adverbial sense and called by some grammarians as *Adverbs of Affirmation.*

जी—is also combined with नहीं—जी नहीं

मत—*Donot.* मत is used with the Imperative. नहीं is not used with Imperative.

CHAPTER XII

Preposition

In Hindī the equivalents of the English prepositions are case-signs and they are used as post-positions. There are very few words besides these case-signs, which are strictly prepositions. Many words which are treated as adverbs. are used as prepositions. Note that such words are used in Hindī after के.

Words used after के.

Hindī.	Eng.	Hindī	Eng.
पास, समीप, निकट, नजदीक, आस-पास	equivalent. *near*	अतिरिक्त, एलावा सिवा	*besides.*
आस-पास	*around, in vicinity*	द्वारा, के द्वारा जरिये	*Through.*
तले, नीचे	*below, beneath*		
पार	*across*	बदले	*for it, in lieu of*
साथ, संगम सहित, समेत	*with*	पहले पूर्व	*before*
भीतर, अन्दर	*in, inside*	कारण, हेतु, सबब	*by reason of,* *on account of*
बाहर आगे सामने	*before, in front,* *in front of*	बिना विना बगैर	*without*
लिये हित अर्थ निमित्त-वास्ते	*for*	एवज बदले	*instead of* *in lieu of*
बाद-पश्चात् अनन्तर-उपरान्त	*after*	बारे में विषय में मारे	*on account of*

Hindi	Eng.
विपरीत विरुद्ध ख़िलाफ	*against*
अनुकूल अनुसार मुताबिक	*according to*

ऊपर— *up, upon*

परे— *beyond*

The following feminine words are used after की :

तरह, भाँति, नाँई—	*like.*
ओर, तरफ—	*towards*
अपेक्षा—	*in comparison to, as compared to*
खातिर—	*for the sake of.*

N.B. If ओर is preceded by a numeral, के comes before it.

सड़क के दोनों ओर	*on both sides of the road.*
सड़क की ओर	*towards the road.*

ओर means *direction* and *extremity* and is noun also. अपेक्षा *'need'* is noun. It is used also to indicate comparison.

Many of such words, serving the purpose of preposition in English, are originally nouns. Perhaps it is the reason why they take के (oblique of का) before them.

Omission of के— तले, पार and द्वारा also come directly after a noun, and का is omitted.

पैरों तले, चिराग तले अँधेरा, नदी पार, समुद्र पार, कृपाण द्वारा, अस्त्र द्वारा।

बिना, सिवा and मारे are ofteu used *before* a noun for the sake of emphasis.

बिना मेरे यह होने का नहीं।	*without me this cannot be done.*
मारे प्यास के जान जा रही थी।	*life was going out on account of* (excessive) *thirst.*

सिवा उसके यह किसी दूसरे का काम नहीं।	*It is the work of none else, but him.*

सहित is often used as second member of a compound; प्रेमसहित *with love,* दयासहित *with kindness.*

We have no simple Hindī equivalents for such words like विरुद्ध, अनुसार, अतिरिक्त and द्वारा. Therefore either these Sanskṛt words are in use or their Urdu equivalents ख़िलाफ़, मुताबिक, एलावा and ज़रिया.

CHAPTER XIII

Conjunction

A conjunction is a word, which joins a word with another word, a sentence with another sentence or joins two parts of a sentence. It is also considered to be an 'Avyaya' by Hindi grammarians. We may classify the conjunctions under the following heads :—

1. *Copulative*— **और** (तथा, एवं) (Sanskṛt) *'and'* फिर (पुनः Sanskṛt) *'again'*, *'moreover'*, *'also'* are also sometimes used in the sense of **और**

2. *Adversative*— पर, परन्तु, किन्तु, लेकिन, *but* मगर, (Ur.) *but*, बल्कि, but, वरन् (Sanskṛt) वर्ना *otherwise.*

3. *Disjunctive.*— या, वा, अथवा (Sanskṛt) *'or'*. Negative disjunctive of नहीं तो *otherwise* शाम को आ जाना नहीं तो भेंट न होगी। *Come in the evening, otherwise we may not meet.* कि— it is also sometimes used as a disjunctive आओगे कि नहीं ? *Will you come or not ?*

न तुम आओ न जाओ इसकी मुझे परवाह नहीं I don't care whether you come or not.

4. *Conditional conjunctive*— जो, यदि (Sk.) अगर (Ur.)

5. *Concessive.* तो *then* यद्यपि (Sanskṛt) *although* गोकि (Ur.) although तथापि (Sanskṛt) *nevertheless.*

6. *Casual conjunction*—कि, क्योंकि, चूँके चूँकि, कारण कि, *because, on account of, owing to* इससे is also used for 'therefore'.

7. *Illative conjunction*—तो *then.*

तुम आओगे तो मुझे चलना ही पड़ेगा—*If you come I will have to go (with you).*

————

CHAPTER XIV

Interjection

An interjection expresses an emotion or feeling (of pleasure, surprise, pain, displeasure, disgust etc.) as अहा ! ओ: आह, हाय, कि Interjections are used as independent words.

The following interjections are commonly in use in Hindī :

(a) ओह ! अरे ! ओहो ! हैं ! क्या ! वाह–	*surprise.*
(b) वाह ! शाबाश ! खूब ! क्या खूब ! धन्य ! जय !	*applause.*
(c) हाय ! हा ! आह ! शोक ! ओफ़ ! उफ़ ! अफ़सोस !	*sorrow, grief.*
(d) अहा ! आहा ! वाह ! वाह वाह !	*joy.*
(e) छि: थू ! धिक् ! धिक्कार !	*disgust.*
(f) हायरे, दैयारे ! बापरे ! बापरे बाप ! माई रे ! मैया रे ! हा राम !	*distress.*
(g) जी ! ठीक ! अच्छा ; शाबाश ! भला !	*affirmation.*
(h) अरे ! अरी ! रे ! री ! अजी ! लो ! जो ! हे !	*vocation.*

Sometimes a verb, a noun, an adjective or an adverb may also be used as an interjection : चल ! हट ! हे राम ! राम राम ! हे भगवान ! अच्छा भला ! खैर ! अस्तु !

Sometimes some interjections are repeated and used as nouns.

चारों ओर हाय-हाय मची । *Everywhere there is cry in grief.*

हम लोग धन्य धन्य हो उठे । *We became pleased or glorified.*

———

SECTION IV

SYNTAX

CHAPTER XV

Syntax

The order and sequence of a word is of importance so that the meaning of a sentence may be clear to the reader. There is a grammatical order of words, and every language has its own rules regarding it.

1. Position of the Nominative

The general rule in Hindī is that the nominative comes first and the verb comes in the end. Other parts of speech, if any, come in between the nominative and the verb. In English the verb generally comes immediately after the nominative and other parts of speech come after the verb.

If the verb meaning 'existence' pure and simple is used, then it comes immediately after the nominative as in English and the sense is complete.

मैं हूँ— *I am* वह है— *He is* (existence is predicated of मैं or वह) मैं था— *I was* वह था— *He was* (existence in past is predicated).

But if anything more than simple existence is predicated, such words come before the verb.

मैं अच्छा हूँ— *I am well.* वह काला है— *He is black.*

(Existence is expressed by the forms of root √ह हूँ , है, हैं, हो)

These are not affected by change of gender of the nominative. Existence in the past is expressed by the forms of root √थ था, थी थीं, थे. When these are not used independently and come as accompanying verb with another verb, both come together at the end of a word.

वह पढ़ता है—	*He reads.*	वह जाता है—	*He goes.*
वह खाता है—	*He eats.*	वह सोता है—	*He sleeps.*

पढ़ता, जाता, खाता and सोता will become पढ़ती, जाती, खाती and सोती if the nominative is feminine, but है will not change. It is necessary to keep this characteristic of verbal forms √ह in mind.

Position of object

2. If the verb is transitive, the object comes in between the noun and the verb.

वह मिठाई खाता है— *He eats sweets.*

वह पुस्तक पढ़ता है— *He reads a book.*

Construction

There are three kinds of constructions (प्रयोग) in Hindi :—

1. Subjectival. 2. Objectival and 3. Neutral.

1. Subjectnal construction (कर्तरि प्रयोग)

मोहन जाता है— *Mohan goes.* सीता जाती है—*Sita goes.*

दो लड़के जाते हैं— *Two boys go.* वह जाता था—*He was going.*

वह जाती थी— *She was going.*

When the subject (Karta) is in direct case the case-sign ने is not attached to it; when ने is attached to the subject, it is in oblique case.)

2. Objectival construction (कर्मणि प्रयोग)

When the subject is in oblique case with ने and the transitive verb is in past participle form, the verb agrees with the object.

राम ने रोटी खाई—*Ram ate bread.* राम ने फल खाये—*Ram ate fruits.*

3. Neutral construction (भावे प्रयोग)

But the verb is always masculine, singular, third person, if को comes after the object or pronoun with ए–हें forms (i. e. मुझे, उसे, हमें, तुम्हें, उन्हें—etc)

लड़कों ने मोहन को अपना नेता बनाया—*The boys made Mohan their leader.*

राम ने मोहन को पढ़ाया हैं—*Ram has taught Mohan.*

उसने मुझे पहचान लिया—*He recognised me.*

सीता ने मुझे अपने घर पर बुलाया है—*Sita has called me at her place.*

At these places the construction is neutral. When the verb is in past participle form, the construction may be either in objectival or neutral construction.

But an intransitive verb must be in subjectival construction, even when it has past participle form.

आम पका है—*The mango is ripe.*

लड़का थका है—*The boy is tired.*

वह घर से आया है—*He has come from house.*

For the purpose of syntax, it is of importance to know whether the construction of a sentence is subjectival, objectival or neutral.

But, where there are two objects, one primary and the other secondary, the secondary object comes before the primary.

गुरु ने मोहन को तर्कशास्त्र पढ़ाया—(The) teacher taught logic to Mohan. तर्कशास्त्र is the primary object and मोहन is secondary object.

3. Position of adjective.

An object comes before the noun or pronoun which it qualifies. However it may come after, and often it is used after the noun (or pronoun). Such use of adjective is considered to be predicative use of the adjective. According to Hindī grammarians this is only 'after. use' (पर प्रयोग) of the adjective.

वह सुन्दर लड़का है— *He is a handsome boy.*

वह लड़का सुन्दर है— †*That boy is handsome.*

If a pronominal or quantitative and an attributive adjective is used together, the former precedes the latter.

---

†. There is more emphasis on the beauty of the boy in the second sentence. The पर प्रयोग (use of adjective after a noun) emphasises the quality or attribute denoted by the adjective.

कोई सुन्दर लड़का आ रहा है— *Some handsome boy is coming.*

कई सुन्दर लड़के आ रहे हैं— *Many handsome boys are coming.*

आठ सुन्दर लड़के आ रहे हैं— *Eight handsome boys are coming.*

4. Extension of the subject and predicate

In a sentence there are two parts—the subject and the predicate. The extension of the subject comes before the subject and that of the predicate, before the predicate.

वह अति तीव्र बुद्धि बालक इस वर्ष परीक्षा में प्रथम श्रेणी पाने की आशा करता है— *That very brilliant boy hopes to get a first class in hts examination this year.*

5. Position of words in Locative, Ablative, Dative and Instrumental cases.

Such words ordinarily come between the nominative and the verb in this order, Locative, Ablative, Dative and Instrumental.

जंगल में जाकर पेड़ से पूजा के लिये कुल्हाड़ी से कुछ लकड़ी काट लाओ ।

Literally translated it is *'going to a jungle cut wood from the tree for worship and bring it'.*

जंगल में— Loc. पेड़से— Abl. पूजा के लिये— Dative
कुल्हाड़ी से— Instru.

6. Often the 'locative of time' comes at the beginning—even before the nomination.

आज मैं घर जा रहा हूं—*Today I am going to home.*

बरसात में सड़क पर निकलना मुश्किल होता है—*In rains it is difficult to move on the road.*

Where there are two locatives one of time and another of place, generally the locative of time comes before the locative of place.

जाड़े में पहाड़ पर बहुत सर्दी पड़ती है—*In winter it is very cold on the hills.*

वर्षा में नदियों में बाढ़ आ जाती है—*In rains flood comes in rivers or During rains rivers are in flood.*

कल मैं तुम्हारे घर आऊँगा—*Tomorrow I will go to your residence.*

Here कल is locative though the case-sign is omitted. कल comes even before the nominative मैं. We may also say मैं कल तुम्हारे घर जाऊँगा but it is quite idiomatic in Hindī to use the locative of time before the nominative. In English the locative of time usually comes at the end—*I will go to your residence tomorrow.*

7. The general rule is that the oblative, the dative and the instrumental come after the nominative, but this is often violated for the sake of emphasis by the speaker.

पेड़ से पत्ते झड़ते हैं। पत्ते पेड़ से झड़ते हैं—*Leaves fall from the tree.*

तुम्हारे लिए मैंने यह टोपी खरीदी है। मैंने तुम्हारे लिये ही टोपी खरीदी है।
I have purchased the cap for you.

Similarly for emphasis, the instrumental may also come at the beginning, It is at the beginning when the verb is in the imperative mood or when the sentence is negative.

कलम से लिखो— *Write by a pen.*

इस हाथ से मैं नहीं लिख सकता— *I cannot write by this hand.*

The vocative comes at the beginning with or without its sign.

हे ईश्वर, तेरी लीला विचित्र है— *O God, your work is wonderful;*

(It is difficult to translate the word 'lila', it has the sense of playful sport.)

For emphasis it may also come at the end—दूर हट बदमाश ! *Get out scoundrel.*

N. B. — The above rules are not strictly followed and may only serve as helpful guides. The normal order of the word is often not observed for emphasis or better style.

CHAPTER XVI

Agreement

Various words in a sentence are related to each other in accordance with certain rules. Generally their relationship takes the following forms :—

1. Relation of verb with the subject or nominative.
2. Relation of verb with the object.
3. Relation of pronoun with noun.
4. Relation of the genetive with the word to which it is related.
5. Relation of adjective with the word qualified by it.

1. Agreement of verb with the nominative or subject

When the nominative is in uninflected form, the verb agrees with it in gender, person and number.

मोहन खाता है— *Mohan eats.* सीता खाती है— *Sita eats.*

मोहन और सोहन खाते हैं— *Mohan and Sohan eat.*

सीता और लीला खाती है— *Sītā and L lā eat.*

मैं खाऊँगा, मैं खाऊँगी— *I shall eat.*

लड़कियाँ जायेंगी— *Girls shall go.*

Note that the verb is not influenced by gender of the nominative in presumptive future.

यदि लड़का खाये, यदि लड़की खाये— *If boy (or girl), eats.*

राम आवे, सीता आवे— *Let Ram come. Let Sītā come.*

When the nominative is in honorofic form the verb takes the plural form आप खाते हैं—*You eat.* स्वामी जी खाते हैं—*Swamiji eats.*

At such places खाता है would be considered undignified also besides being incorrect.

When there are two or more nominatives and all are of the same gender, number and person then the verb will take plural form of the same gender.

राम, श्याम, गोपाल और गोरख एक ही शिक्षक से पढ़ते हैं— *Ram, Shyam, Gopal and Gorakh read 'from' the same teacher (are taught by the same teacher).*

But if two abstract nouns are in the nominative, the verb may take singular form.

आनन्द और सुख सब को नहीं मिलते or नहीं मिलता।

Bliss and pleasure is not given to all (All do not have bliss and pleasure).

When there are two nominatives, differing in gender (whether joined by a conjunctive or not) the verb generally takes masculine plural form.

1. मेरे भाई बहन मर चुके हैं— or मेरे भाई और बहन मर चुके हैं— *My brother and sister are dead.*

2. नेपाल के राजारानी दिल्ली आये हैं—*The king and queen of Nepal have arrived in Delhi.*

3. नरेश और उसकी पत्नी सिनेमा देखने गये हैं—*Naresh and his wife have gone to Cinema.*

4. शीला और शेखर पटने में पढ़ते हैं—*Şilá and Şekhar read at Patna.*

But when there are several nominatives, some mas. and some fem., and the last nom. comes after और, the verb may agree with the nom. nearest to it.

आजकल मेरे घर में चार पुरुष, दस बच्चे और सात स्त्रियाँ आई हैं—*Four men, ten children and seven ladies have come at my house these days.*

जवाहरलाल जी के स्वागत में बालक-वृद्ध, स्त्री-पुरुष, गरीब-अमीर और छोटे-बड़े सभी उपस्थित थे—*Boys and old people, ladies and gentlemen, the poor and the rich and small and big persons – all were present to welcome Jawaharlalji.*

At such places words like सभी or सब are after used before the last nominative.

बैल, गाय, हाथी, घोड़े और तरह-तरह की चिड़ियाँ सोनपुर मेले में बिकने को आई थीं—*Oxen, cows, elephants, horses and birds of various kinds had come for sale in the Sonepore fair.*

राम को धोती, कुरता और टोपी फट गई हैं—*Ram's dhotī, Kurtā and cap are torn.*

When nominatives are generally arranged according to the reverse order—i. e. third, second and first person, the verb agrees with the last.

वह, तुम और मैं वहाँ जाऊँगा—*He, you and I shall go there.*

वह और तुम वहाँ जाओ—*He and you go there.*

तुम और मैं बाज़ार चलूँ—*You and me go to the bazar.*

भाभी और तुम सिनेमा देख सकते हो—*Bhabhi (elder's brother's wife) and you may go to see cinema.*

पिताजी और मैं कलकत्ता जाऊँगा—*Papa and I shall go to Calcutta.*

If the subjects are of three different persons, then the verb will be of third person मैं, तुम और वह जायेंगे—*I, you and he will go.*

If the subject is third person and first person the verb will be first person मोहन और मैं जाऊँगा—If the subject is in second and third person the verb will be of second person तुम और वह खा रहे हो।

Personal pronouns are joined by conjunctive और.

When two or more nominatives are in different numbers, and the last is an oblique case (a case other than the nominative case) with its case-sign, the previous nominatives require no case-sign.

सोनपुर मेले में हाथी, घोड़े, बैल, गाय, हिरन, और नाना भाँति के पक्षियों का दृश्य बड़ा लुभावना होता है—

The scene of elephants, horses, bullocks, deers and various kinds of birds is very pleasing or attractive in the Sonepur fair.

If nominatives are joined by disjunctive या (अथवा) then the verb agrees with the nominative nearest to it.

मैं या तुम जाओगे— *I or you will go.*

तुम या मैं जाऊँगा— *You or I will go.*

तुम, मैं या वह जायेगा— *You, I or he will go.*

There are two forms of nominative in Hindī, one pure nominative form, where no case-sign is attached, and the second, where case-sign ने is used. This ने must be used in all tenses formed from the perfect participle of th e transitive verbs.

2. Agreement of verb with the object

When ने is used after the nominative, the transitive verb agrees with the object (with its case sign को)

But when object with its case-sign को is used the verb always takes masculine singular form.

1. लड़के ने यह तस्वीर देखी है— *The boy has seen this picture (obejct-fem. sing.)*

   लड़की ने यह तस्वीर देखी है—*The girl ,, ,, ,, ,,*

2. लड़के ने ये तस्वीरें देखी हैं— *The boy has seen the pictures (object-fem. plu.)*

   लड़की ने ये तस्वीरें देखी हैं— *The girl ,, ,, ,, ,,*

3. लड़के ने यह चित्र देखा है— *The boy has seen this picture (object-masc.sig.)*

   लड़की ने यह चित्र देखा है— *The girl ,, ,, ,, ,,*

4. लड़कों ने ये चित्र देखे हैं— *The boys have seen these pictures.*

   लड़कियों ने ये चित्र देखे हैं— *The girls ,, ,, ,, ,,*

This is called 'objectival construction' because the verb agrees with the object.

Object with को

When the object is with its case-sign को, the verb will be in the past tense and third person mas. sing.

लड़के ने इस चित्र को देखा है— *The boy has seen this picture (Object. mas. sing.)*

लड़की ने इस चित्र को देखा है— *The girl ,, ,, ,, ,,*

लड़के ने इस तस्वीर को देखा है—*The boy ,, ,, ,, ,,* (*Object. fem. sing.*)

लड़की ने इस तस्वीर को देखा है—*The girl ,, ,, ,, ,,*

लड़कों ने इस तस्वीर को देखा है—*The boys have ,, ,, ,,*

लड़कियों ने इस तस्वीर को देखा है—*The girls ,, ,, ,,*

देखा है will also be used if चित्र or तस्वीर (picture) is used in plural. Thus we see that when को is used with the object, the verb is always in third person masculine singular form.

This is Neutral Construction as here the verb neither agrees with the object, nor with the subject.

In Impersonal voice, specially in a negative sentence, the transitive verb is always in the third person mas. sing. form.

लड़के से, लड़कों से, लड़की से व लड़कियों से अब चला नहीं जाता।

The boy, boys, girl or girls cannot move now. (translation is in active voice).

मोहन से या लीला से अब खाया नहीं जाता—*Mohan or Lilā cannot eat now.*

Mark that the subject is always with से in such sentences and is neutral construction. *.

When there are two objects, one primary and the other sencondary the verb agrees with the primary object.

1. राम ने मोहन को चिट्ठी लिखी है—*Ram has written a letter to Mohan.* चिट्ठी *(letter)* is fem. so the verb is fem.

राम ने मोहन को पत्र लिखा है—*Ram has written a letter to Mohan.* पत्र *(letter)* is mas., so the verb is fem.

चिट्ठी or पत्र is primary object and Mohan is secondarv object.

*. See the chapter on voice and construction in Hindi

2. मोहन को एक रुपया दिया गया—*One rupee was given to Mohan.*
मोहन को चार रुपये दिये गये—*Four rupees were given to Mohan.*

एक रुपया or चार रुपये is primary object and मोहन secondary object.

3. Agrement of pronoun with noun

The pronoun agrees with the noun for which it comes, as regards person and number.

राम ने कहा कि मैं आऊँगा— *Ram said that he would come.*

लड़कों ने कहा कि हम शाम को आवेंगे –*The boys said that they would come in the evening.*

Note that in Hindī the exact words of the speaker is introduced by कि.

It is bad form of Hindī to say राम ने कहा कि वह आवेगा or लड़कों ने कहा कि वे शाम को आवेंगे। Such constructions are influenced by English language.

4. Agreement of the Genetive with the word to which it is related

The Genetive is called सम्बन्ध in Hindī. The form of the Genetive case-sign depends on the gender and number of the word following, to which it is related in different senses.

The genetive may denote 'possession'—as मोहन का घर *the house of Mohan or Mohan's house; 'relationship.'* मोहन का भाई *brother of Mohan; 'material'* चाँदी का गहना *ornament of silver; 'place'* काशी का पंडित-*a pandit of Kaśi 'origin or source'* हिमालय की नदियाँ *the rivers of the Himalayas, 'age;'* चार साल का लड़का *a boy of four years. 'cause'* भूख का मारा *weary of hunger, 'quality or kind.'* खेद की बात—*a matter of sorrow, 'of use or purpose'* पाने का पानी *water for drinking or drinking water, 'time'*—कल का समाचार *news of yesterday; Price*— एक रुपये का आम *mango for a rupee etc.*

If the following word, whose relation with the previous word is denoted, is mas. sing. the case-sign का is used. If the preceding word is pronoun मैं or तुम its genetive form will be मेरा or तुम्हारा and if it is आप (self) it will be अपना and if आप (honorific) it will be आपका.

राम का घर—	*Ram's house.*	मेरा घर—	*My house.*
तुम्हारा घर—	*Your house.*	अपना घर—	*My own house.*
आप का घर—	*Your (honorofic sense) house.*		

If the word following is mas. plural, the case-sign will be के, with reflexive आप it will be नें and will मैं and तुम will be रे *.

ये राम के घर हैं— *These are Ram's houses.*
ये मेरे घर हैं— *These are my houses.*
ये अपने घर हैं— *These are my own houses.*

If the word following is feminine singular or plural, की is used after preceding nouns.

राम की घड़ी या घड़ियाँ *Ram's watch or watches* री with मैं and हम तुम and नी with reflexive आप.

मेरी घड़ी या घड़ियाँ— *My watch or watches.*
हमारी घड़ी या घड़ियाँ— *Our watch or watches.*
तुम्हारी घड़ी या घड़ियाँ— *Our watch or watches.*
अपनी घड़ी या घड़ियाँ— *My own watch or watches.*

If the following noun is masculine and in the oblique case and with case-sign, का becomes के, ना become ने aud रा becomes रे.

सीता के घर को, घर से, घर पर, घर में।
अपने लड़के को, लड़के से, लड़के पर, लड़के में।

In the above sentences the words घर and लड़के is singular.

---

*. We may regard क and न as three letters which are used in forming genetive signs. क assumes का form in mas. sing., की in fem. and के in mas. plur. न is used only with reflexive आप and assumes ना, नी, ने. forms र is used only with pronouns मैं, हम and तुम—मेरा, मेरी, मेरे, हमारा; हमारी, हमारे. तुम्हारा, तुम्हारी, तुम्हारे।

If different nouns are related to the subject genetically, the genetive case-sign will be determined by the gender and number of the first noun following.

राम की पत्नी, लड़के, भाई, बहन सभी आज सिनेमा गये थे ।
Ram's wife, sons, brothers and sisters all had gone to Cinema,

Here की is used as पत्नी is feminine.

If लड़के is placed first it will be like this.

राम के लड़के, पत्नी, भाई, बहिन सभी आज सिनेमा गये थे ।

Agreement of adjective with the word qualified by it

An adjective may be used either attributively or predicatively. Generally it precedes a noun it qualifies. It is often used after the noun and then is said to be used predicatively.

वह सुन्दर लड़की है—*She is a beautiful girl* or वह लड़की सुन्दर है—*The girl is beautiful.* Here the adjective सुन्दर is used predicatively.

When several adjectives, qualifying the same noun (or pronoun), the last two are joined by a conjunctive.

वह बहुत बड़ा विद्वान्, परिश्रमी और महत्त्वाकांक्षी है ।
He is a great scholar, industrious and ambitious (man)

गांधीजी महान्, त्यागी, तपस्वी और देशभक्त थे ।
Gandhiji was great, self-sacrificing, saintly and a patriot.

Masculine and feminine forms of adjectives.

An adjective may have two forms, one masculine and the other feminine or it may have only one form which is used with both masc. and fem. nouns.

Thus Sanskṛt सुन्दर, मधुर, सरस—become सुन्दरी, मधुरा, सरसा—in fem. अच्छा, बुरा, काला become अच्छी, बुरी, काली in fem. and अच्छे, बुरे and काले in Mas. plural. or in oblique cases.

Mas.	Fem.	Mas. Plul.
सुन्दर बालक	सुन्दरी बालिका	
मधुर फल	मधुर वाणी	

सरस व्यवहार	सरसा प्रकृति	
अच्छा लड़का	अच्छी लड़की	अच्छे लड़के
बुरा काम	बुरी बात	बुरे काम
काला आदमी	काली औरत	काले आदमी

Hindī does not follow strictly the Sanskṛt rule that an adjective should necessarily assume its feminine form, when qualifying a feminine noun. Thus सुन्दर कन्या is correct in Hindī and it is not necessary to write सुन्दरी कन्या, The adjective may be in masculine form even when it qualifies a feminine यह बड़ी मधुर (or सरस) कविता है *This is a very sweet poem.* But a feminine adjective can not be used before a mas. noun. वह सुन्दरी बालक है can never be tolerated in Hindī.

Many non-Sanskṛt adjectives have two forms--mas. and fem. —and they should be in agreement with the noun following as regards gender. There are few adjectives which have no corresponding feminine forms. They may be treated as adjectives of common gender—ex. बढ़िया, घटिया, तेज़, क़ाबिल, लाल, असलो, फ़सली.

Of these many are Urdū (Persian or Arabic) adjectives.

Thus, we have

(Mas.)	(Fem.)
बढ़िया घी	बढ़िया किताब
घटिया माल	घटिया साटी
लाल कपड़ा	लाल टोपी
तेज़ लड़का	तेज़ लड़की
असली काम	असली बात
फ़सली आम	फ़सली बीमारी

When there are many nouns of different genders and numbers, the adjective agrees with the noun immediately following.

नरेश की काली टोपी, चश्मा और कपड़े यहीं छूट गये थे।
Naresh's black cap, spectacles and clothes were left here.

Adjectives ending in आ have feminine forms ending in ई.

अच्छा–अच्छी	काला–काली	पीला–पीली
गोरा–गोरी	सुनहला–सुनहली	उजला–उजली
दसवाँ–दसवीं	बायाँ–बायीं	दाहिना–दाहिनी

All such adjectives have ए–ending forms in mas. plur. and oblique cases.

अच्छे लड़के ने—	(से, को, में, पर etc.)
गोरे लड़के ने —	(से, को, में, पर ,,)
काले लड़के ने —	(से, को, में, पर ,,)
पीले लड़के ने—	(से, को, में, पर ,,)

Similarly दसवें, बायें, दाहिने, उजले, सुनहले with case-signs. दसवें दरजे मे, बायें हाथ को, दाहिने हाथ से, उजले कपड़े पर, सुनहरे रंग को are used.

These ए—forms are very important and should be carefully used. Mistakes of this kind are made by speakers whose mother-tongue is not Hindī. Therefore be careful in using the proper form of adjectives in आ.

छोटा लड़का से बोल दो। (लड़के से)—*Tell the little boy.*

दाहिना हाथ को दिखलाओ। (दाहिने)—*Show your right hand.*

तुम्हारा स्कूल में कौन हेडमास्टर है। (तुम्हारे)—*Who is the headmaster in your School ?*

तुम्हारा पीछे में मैं गया था (तुम्हारे) I had gone after you. पीछे and not पीछे में

Use of सा (सी, से)

सा gives the idea of resemblance and is accompanied with the idea of a lesser degree of quality.

हरा-सा कपड़ा— *Green-like cloth.* गुलाब-सा मुखड़ा— a rose—like face, गोल-सा चेहरा— *Circle-like face* (a circular face) It also is changed to सी and से forms and is treated like the adjectives पीली-सी सारी, लम्बी-सी छड़ी *Yellow-like Sari* and *long-like stick.*

'Yellow'-like Sari.' 'and' 'long-like stick' Literal translations are given here to show the Hindī constructions. काली-सी सारी would mean *'a Sari having a resembling yellow colour'*. long-like stick' would mean *'a stick which is similar to a long stick.'*

When सा (सी, से) comes after का (की, के) it denotes likeness, not with the person or thing, but with something, pertaining to the person or thing coming before का. Thus राच्तस का सा चेहरा (राच्तस के चेहरे के समान) means *'a face like that of a demon'* हाथों के से दाँत— means *'a tooth like that of an elephant'* and जानवर की सी-बोली—means *'voice resembling that of an animal.'*

सा also sometimes denotes excess or degree of anything or quality बहुत-सा जलपान— *'a good refreshment'* जरा-सा घाव *'a little abscess'*, थोड़ा सा भोजन *'a little food.'* मुझे बहुत-सी बातें करनी है *I have to talk a great deal.*

At such places the sense of resemblance is quite absent, only degree or quantity is denoted.

This सा (सी, से) is always hyphened with the preceding word. सा is commonly used in Hindī to give a sense of resemblance or similarity and in grammar treated as an adjective.

SECTION V

FORMATION OF WORDS BY PREFIXES AND SUFFIXES.

SANDHI, SAMĀSA. PUNCTUATION IN HINDĪ.

CHAPTER XVII

Formation of words by Prefixes and Suffixes.

A large number of words in any language are formed by the process of appending prefixes or suffixes to verbal roots or other words. Sanskṛt grammarians give the following 22 prefixes, which when used with a root or another word, considerably change their meaning. Sometimes these prefixes (उपसर्ग) change the meaning of the root, intensify or diminish it or leave it unaffected or alter the meaning.

Sanskṛt Prefixes

प्र, प्रा, अप, सम अनु, अव निस्, निर्, दुस्, दुर्, अभि, वि, आँङ् (आ) नि अधि, अपि, सु, उत्, अति, प्रति परि, उप।

प्र—It expresses the idea of (1) *motion* (2) *excellence* and (3) *increased degree.*

प्रस्थान, प्रयोग, प्रणाम, प्रधान, प्रचार, प्रकार, प्रसाद, प्रमेय, प्रहार, प्रदान, प्रबल।

परा— (1) *reversal* as in पराजय

(2) *excellence* as in पराक्रम

(3) *disregard*— परास्त,

पराभव, पराकाष्ठा, परामर्श, परावर्तन।

अप— (1) *taking away* as in अपमान

(2) *inferiority*— अपदेवता, अपव्यय

अपराध, अपवाद, अपशकुन, अपहरण, अपशब्द, अपभ्रन्श, अपयश, अपरूप, अपादान,

सम्— (1) *union*, as in संयोग, संसर्ग

(2) *completeness* — सन्तुष्ट,

सम्राट, संभाषण, संभ्रम, संवाद, संविधान, संशय

अनु— (1) *after*, as in अनुचर

(2) *similarity* as in अनुरूप,

अनुकरण, अनुवाद, अनुसरण, अनुमान, अनुभव

अव— (1) *disrespect* as in अवगुण

(2) *down*— अवतीर्ण

(3) *intensive sense* also — अवशेष,

अवरोध, अवसान, अवदान, अवधान ।

निर्— (1) *absence* as in निराकार

निस्— (2) *certainty* as in निर्धारण,

निस्सार, निस्तेज, निश्चल,

निरर्थक, निर्मूल्य, निरपराध, निराधार ।

दुर्— (1) *difficulty* as in दुष्कर

दुस्— (2) *deterioration*, as in दुर्दशा,

दुर्गम, दुस्तर, दुर्नाम, दुर्दैव,

अभि— (1) *towards*, अभिमुख ।

(2) *thoroughness* or *expressed clearly*—अभिनव, अभिव्यक्त

अभियान, अभिचार, अभिवादन, अभिराम, अभिचार ।

वि— (1) *separation* as in वियोग

(2) *opposition* विमुख, विवाद

(3) *intensive sense* विभाग,

विन्यास, विधान, विलास, विकल, विचार, विनिमय ।

अधि— (1) *superiority* as in अधिराज

(2) *up* as in अधित्यका,

अधिकार, अधिकरण, अधिवास, अधि-पति, अधिमास ।

सु— It gives the idea of *good*, *easy*, *happy* as in सुशील, सुवास, सुभाष, सुधार, सुकुमार, सुयोग, सुगम ।

उत्— (1) *upwards* as in उदय

(2) *excellence* as in उद्योग,

उद्गम, उन्मूलन, उद्घाटन, उद्विग्न, उद्वेग, उद्भव ।

अति— (1) *excess* as in अत्युक्ति, अतिवृष्टि, अतिशय, अतिसार, अतीव ।

नि— (1) *sense of completeness* as in निमग्न, निवारण, निरूपण, निदान, नियोग, निधान ।

प्रति— (1) *opposition* as in प्रतिकूल, प्रतिपक्ष
(2) *return* as in प्रतिदान, प्रत्युपकार
(3) *every* प्रत्येक

This prefix is also used separately as a word

परि— It gives the idea of (1) *all round* as in परिधि, परिक्रमा, परिभ्रमण
(2) *blame* as in परिहास
(3) *succession* as in परिच्छेद,

परितोष, परिताप, परिमाण, परिवहन, परिचय ।

उप—It gives (1) the idea of *nearness*, as in उपनिषद् , उपकूल ।
(2) *sub*—or *deputy* or *vice*—उपराष्ट्रपति, उपमंत्री, उपचार, उपराम, उपकार, उपयोग, उपवास ।

आ— It gives (1) the sense of *extension of*, *upto*, as in आजानु ।
(2) sometimes it has the sense of 'slight', as in आशंका ।
(3) sense of *opposite* as in आगमन ।

Besides the above prefixes many Sanskṛt words (adj. and indeclinables) are also used as prefixes.

अ— *absence*, *less* अज, अगाध, अज्ञ, अपार, असार, अभाव, अकाल, असुर, अन्याय Before words with initial vowel—this अ becomes अन्—अनन्त, अनादि, अनाचार, अनाहार, अनशन ।

अन्तर्—(अंत:)—*inter*—अन्तर्जातीय, अन्तर्प्रान्तीय. अन्तर्गत = अन्तर्गत, अन्तर्द्वार ।

प्राक्— *before*—*pre* प्राक् ऐतिहासिक, प्रागैतिहासिक, प्राक्कथन ।

पुनर्— *again*—*'re'* पुनर्जन्म, पुनर्भव, पुनरुत्थान (पुन: उत्थान), पुनर्विवाह, पुनरुक्ति ।

स— (*with*) सफल, सजातीय, सकुशल, सहर्ष।

सह— (*with, together*) सहगमन, सहयोग, सहकारी, सहपाठी, सहधर्मिणी।

सत्— *good* सत्जन (सज्जन), सत्गुरु (सद्गुरु), सत्+आचार=सदाचार सत् धर्म=सद्धर्म, सत्भाव (सद्भाव)।

स्व— *self* स्वराज्य, स्वगत, स्वाधीन, स्वदेश, स्वभाव।

स्वयं— *Voluntarily, by se'f* स्वयंसेवक, स्वयंवर, स्वयम्, स्वयंसिद्ध।

पुरस्— *in front, onward* पुरस्कार, पुरश्चरण।

प्रादुर्— *to appear* प्रादुर्भाव।

बहिर्— *outside* बहिर्गत, बहिष्कार, बहिर्मुख।

न— *absence*, negative sense नग, नपुंसक, नास्तिक।

चिर्— *very, excess*—चिरायु, चिरंजीव, चिरकाल।

तिरस्— *to consider low*—तिरस्कार, तिरोभाव।

अधस्— *below*—अधोगति, अधःपतन, अधोमुख।

Hindī Prefixes

These prefixes are added to pure Hindī or tadbhava words.

अ— *absence*—अजान, अथाह, अपच।

अन्— *without*—अनजान, अनपढ़, अनमोल, अनबन।

अध— *half*. (from अर्ध Sanskṛt) अधखिला, अधपका, अधसेरा, अधजला।

उन— *less one*. (from Sanskṛt) उनतीस, उनसठ, उन्नीस, उनहत्तर। It is generally prefixed to numerals.

दु— *bad*. दुकाल, दुबला।

नि— *absence of, without* निडर, निधड़क, निकम्मा, निलज।

भर— } भरपूर, भरमार. भरसक।

कु— } *bad* कुडौल, कुढंग।

क— कपूत।

सु— *good* सुडौल, सुजान, सुघड़।

Urdū Prefixes

कम— *small, less*. कमजोर, कमसिन, कमकीमत।

खुश— *good, pleasant.* खुशबू , खुशहाल, खुशनसीब, खुशमिजाज ।

ग़ैर— *without, not,* ग़ैरहाजिर, ग़ैरसरकारी, ग़ैरमुमकिन ।

दर— *in, between* दरअसल, दरहक़ीक़त, दरपेशी ।

ना— *absence, without* नादान, नालायक, नामुमकिन, नापसंद ।

ब— *in, with* बनाम, बदौलत, बइजलास ।

बद— *bad* बदनाम, बदबू, बदक़िस्मत, बदतमीज़ ।

बर— *upon, at* बरवक़्त, बरतरफ़ ।

बा— *with* बाकायदा, बाजाब्ता, बाकलम ।

बिला— *without* बिलाअक्ल, बिलाशक ।

बे— *without* बेईमान, बेइंसाफ़, बेवकूफ़, बेरहम, बेहोश ।
Sometimes it is also used with Hindī words. बेजोड़, बेडौल, बेकाम ।

ला— *without* लाचार, लावारिस, लाजवाब, लापरवाह ।

सर— *main* सरनाम, सरताज, सरकार ।
It is also added with पंच a Hindī word, सरपंच ।

हम-- *with, same* हमदर्द, हमउम्र, हमराह ।

Suffixes (प्रत्यय)

Sanskṛt suffixes.

Here only such suffixes of Sanskṛt are given which are used in Sanskṛt words (mainly nouns). The formation of Sanskṛt words like भाव, दान really comes in the domain of Sanskṛt grammar.

These suffixes may be classed under two heads, verbal suffixes (कृदन्त) and nominal suffixes. (तद्धित)

Sanskṛt nominal suffixes (तद्धित)

अ— (*son of*) रघु--राघव, कुरु -- कौरव, पाण्डु--पाण्डव

वसुदेव—वासुदेव, पर्वत — पार्वती (*daughter of Parvata*) मनु--मानव, दनु—दानव, सुमित्रा—सौमित्र, कश्यप—काश्यप, शिव—शैव, (*worshipper of Shiva*) विष्णु—वैष्णव

It also means *possession, quality of* चन्द्र—चान्द्र, पृथिवी—पार्थिव, व्याकरण—वैयाकरण (*grammarian*) निशि—नैश, सूर—सौर

Other suffixes meaning *'son of'*

य—दिति—दैत्य

एय—राधा–राधेय, विनता—वैनतेय, गंगा—गांगेय ।

Suffix meaning *'father of'*

मह—मातामह, पितामह, प्रपितामह ।

Suffixes forming abstract nouns (masc.)

अ—मुनि—मौन

अव्—लघु—लाघव, गुरु—गौरव ।

त्व—पुरुषत्व, महत्—महत्व, तत्त्व—तत्त्व

य—पंडित—पाण्डित्य, वणिज, वाणिज्य, धीर—धैर्य, स्वस्थ स्वास्थ्य

Suffixes forming adjectives

आलु—कृपा—कृपालु, दया—दयालु, श्रद्धा—श्रद्धालु, हृदय हृदयालु, निद्रालु ।

इक—मूल—मौलिक, मुख—मौखिक, नाव—नाविक, दिन–दैनिक, एक—ऐकिक, समुद्र—सामुद्रिक, लोक—लौकिक, मास—मासिक, स्वर्ग—स्वार्गिक, संकेत सांकेतिक, वर्ष—वार्षिक, देह—दैहिक, इतिहास—ऐतिहासिक, विधान—वैधानिक,

(N.B. when इक is added, the initial vowel takes its Vṛddhi form अ--आ, इ--ऐ--उ--औ ।

इत—दुःख—दुखित, चिन्ता—चिन्तित, फल फलित, कल्प—कल्पित, इच्छा—इच्छित, परीक्षा—परीक्षित, उपेक्षा—उपेक्षित ।

---

*. Hindī has adopted Sanskṛt words as स्मरण, पूजन, करण, कथन, आदर as loan words of Sanskṛt. How these words are formed from roots स्मृ, पूज्, कृ, कथ् आ+दृ, कथ् etc. are to be studied in a Sanskṛt Grammar.

इल—फेन—फेनिल, तंद्र—तंद्रिल, तुंद—तुंदिल, जटा—जटिल, स्वप्न—स्वप्निल,
पंक—पंकिल ।

इम—रक्त—रक्तिम, अन्त—अन्तिम, अग्र—अग्रिम ।

इष्ठ—गुरु—गरिष्ठ, वर—वरिष्ठ, बल—बलिष्ठ ।

ई— प्रणय—प्रणयी, धन—धनी, गुण—गुणी, रोग—रोगी, वाद—वादी ।

ईन—कुल - कुलीन, ग्राम—ग्रामीण, नव—नवीन ।
काल—कालीन, शाल—शालीन ।

ईय—मानव—मानवीय, देश—देशीय, प्रांत—प्रांतीय ।
स्वर्ग—स्वर्गीय, पुस्तक—पुस्तकीय, नरक—नारकीय, मनन—मननीय,
चिन्तन—चिन्तनीय ।

उक—भाव—भावुक, भिक्षा—भिक्षुक, इच्छा—इच्छुक ।

क— हिंस—हिंसक, दाह—दाहक, मोद—मोहक, पाल—पालक ।

कीय—राज—राजकीय, स्व—स्वकीय, पर—परकीय ।

निष्ठ—विचारनिष्ठ, कर्मनिष्ठ ।

तन—अद्यतन, पुरातन, नूतन, चिरंतन ।

म— आदि—आदिम, मध्य—मध्यम, प्रथ—प्रथम ।

मान् (मती)—श्रीमान्, श्रीमती, आयुष्मान्, आयुष्मती ।

वान्—गुणवान—गुणवती ।

र— मधु—मधुर, मुख—मुखर, नख—नखर ।

ल— मृदु—मृदुल, मंजु—मंजुल, मांस—मांसल ।
श्याम, श्यामल ।

वी—तेजस्—तेजस्वी, मनस्—मनस्वी ।

मय—सुखमय, आनन्दमय, जलमय, विष्णुमय ।

Suffixes meaning 'manner'

धा— द्विधा, बहुधा, शतधा ।

था— तथा, यथा, सर्वथा, अन्यथा ।

शः क्रमशः, अल्पशः, अक्षरशः, कोटिशः ।

तः— प्रथमतः, सम्भवतः, अंशतः, स्वतः ।

Sanskṛt suffixes forming abstract noun

अना— विद्—वेदना, घट् —घटना, रच्—रचना ।
तुल्—तुलना, सूच्—सूचना, आ+राध्=आराधना ।

आ— इष् (इच्छ्)=इच्छ्+आ=इच्छा ।
पूज्+आ=पूजा, क्रीड्+आ=क्रीडा, व्यथ्+आ=व्यथा ।

क्ति— शक्+क्ति=शक्ति, भज्+क्ति=भक्ति ।

ति— कृ+ति=कृति, प्री+ति=प्रीति, स्मृ+ति=स्मृति

In many words ending in न् and म्, न् म is dropped before
ति, मन्—मति, गम्—गति, रम्—रति, पम्—पति ।

नि— हा+नि=हानि, ग्ला+नि=ग्लानि ।

इमा— महत्—महिमा, गुरु—गरिमा, अरुण—अरुणिमा, नील—नीलिमा ।

ता— महत्—महत्ता, गुरु—गुरुता, लघु—लघुता, सम—समता ।

A large number of words are used as suffixes in Sanskṛt words. They are never used as words separately. A list of such common words are given below.

अर्ह— (*worthy of*) पूजार्ह, दंडार्ह ।

आवह— (*having the quality of*) हितावह, सुखावह ।

आढ्य— (*full of*) गुणाढ्य बलाढ्य, धनाढ्य ।

कर— (*doer of*) दिनकर, दिवाकर, निशाकर, प्रभाकर, हितकर, सुखकर, आनन्दकर ।

कार— (*maker of, worker of*) चर्मकार, शिल्पकार, कुंभकार, स्वर्णकार, नाटककार, उपन्यासकार ।

---

*. For the purpose of Hindi language, in my opinion these words are borrowed from Sanskṛt. To understand the formation of such words, it is necessary to know Sanskṛt roots and rules of Sanskṛt grammar.

कालीन— (*of the time or period of*) पूर्वकालीन, समकालीन, पुराकालीन, जन्मकालीन ।

ग— (*goer*) नग, अग, खग, दुर्ग, तुरग, उरग ।

गम— (*which goes*) सुगम, अगम, दुर्गम, आगम ।

ज्ञ— (*knower of*) विज्ञ, अज्ञ, सर्वज्ञ, नीतिज्ञ, अभिज्ञ, शास्त्रज्ञ ।

घ्न— (*killer of*) शत्रुघ्न, कृतघ्न, पादघ्न ।

ज— (*born of*) जलज, पंकज, नीरज, स्वेदज, अनुज, पिंडज, द्विज, जारज ।

जीवी— (*leading life of*) श्रमजीवी, दीर्घजीवी, तृणजीवी ।

द— (*giver of*) जलद, नीरद, धनद, दुःखद, सुखद ।

दायक— } (*giver of*) आनन्ददायक, सुखदायक ।
दायी— } आनन्ददायी, सुखदायी ।

धर— (*keeper of*) श्रीधर, मुरलीधर, विद्याधर, गंगाधर, जलधर, गिरिधर, भूधर ।

शाली— (*possessing or having*) गुणशाली, भाग्यशाली, ऐश्वर्यशाली ।

स्थ— (*living in, standing in*) गृहस्थ, मध्यस्थ, तटस्थ, अंतःस्थ, उदरस्थ ।

हर— (*remover of*) दुःखहर, रोगहर ।

हारी— तापहारी,श्रमहारी ।

Some Suffixes forming adverbs or indeclinables

दा— Signifying *time*. एकदा, सर्वदा, सदा, तदा ।

त्र— Signifying *place*. तत्र, यत्र, एकत्र, सर्वत्र ।

चित्— क्वचित, कदाचित, कश्चित् ।

Hindī Suffixes

Suffixes are added to roots, nouns, pronouns or adjectives to form new words.

These suffixes may be classified under the following principal heads.

(1) Suffixes which are added to roots to form verbal nouns or adjectives etc. These are called primary suffixes (*Kridant*).

(2) Suffixes which are added to a noun or adjective to form again nouns and adjectives. These are called secondary suffixes (*taddhit*).

These suffixes form the following classes of words :—

1. *Patronymics.* जा—भतीजा, भानजा ।
2. *Gentiles.* ई—बिहार-बिहारी, बंगाल-बंगाली ।
3. *Agentives.* वाला, हारा—बोलनेवाला, सुननेवाला, लकड़हारा ।
4. *Nouns indicative of a holder or container* औटी-चुनौटी ।
5. *Abstract nouns.* आई, त, वट—बुराई, रंगाई, रंगत, दिखावट, बुनावट ।
6. *Diminutives.* इया—डिबिया, लुटिया, डी—पगड़ी, टँगड़ी ।
7. *Adjectives.* आऊ—बिकाऊ, ईली—लजीला, सजीला, कबीला ।
8. *Suffixes forming fem. from mas.* इन, आइन—धोबिन, ठकुराइन ।
9. *Suffixes forming mas. from fem.* ओई—बहनोई, नंनदोई ।
10. *Suffixes forming infinitives* and participial form. ना, ता—पढ़ना, पढ़ता ।

N. B. Many sufflxes are both primary and secondary. The same suffix may be used in more than one sense.

Suffixes forming abstract nouns (भाववाचक संज्ञा के प्रत्यय)

अ— मर-मार, चल-चाल, मिल-मेल ।
Initial vowel is changed to its guṇa form (इ-ए, उ-ओ) ।

आ— mas. घेरा, फेर-फेरा ।

आई— fem. लड़-लड़ाई, जोत-जुताई, सींच-सिंचाई, पैर-पैराई, देख-देखाई, लिख-लिखाई ।

ए in पैराई is not fully pronounced. Initial ए and ओ and ई is changed to its short form इ and उ after this suffix. Mark that जोत becomes जुत, सींच becomes सिंच ।

with adjectives ढीठ-ढिठाई, बड़ा-बड़ाई, भला-भलाई,

with nouns पंडित-पंडिताई, ठाकुर-ठकुराई ।

आप—mas. मिल-मिलाप ।

आपा—बूढ़ा - बुढ़ापा, मोटा - मोटापा or मुटापा ओ in मो is slightly pronounced. The tendency to prefer इ and उ to partly pronounced ए and ओ is growing in Hindī, perhaps as there is no special sign for denoting the short pronunciation of ए and ओ. ॆ ॊ signs for short ए and ओ sounds are suggested.

आव—	mas.	खींच-खिंचाव, बीच-बिचाव ।
आवा—	mas.	देख-दिखावा, बोल-बुलावा ।
आवट—	fem.	मेल-मिलावट, देख-दिखावट
औता—	mas.	समझ-समझौता
औती—	fem.	मान-मनौती, बाप-बपौती, चुन-चुनौती, बूढ़ा,बुढ़ौती
औवा—	mas.	बूझ-बुझौवल
इ—	fem.	हंस-हंसी, बोल-बोली । with nouns दलाल-दलाली, सुनार-सुनारी, महाजन-महाजनी
त—	fem.	बच-बचत
ती—	fem.	चढ़-चढ़ती, बढ़-बढ़ती
न्ती—		चढ़-चढ़न्ती, बढ़-बढ़न्ती ।
न — नी—	fem.	दे-देन, ले-लेन, रह-रहन, चट-चटनी, कट-कटनी, माँग-मँगनी, with nouns चांद-चादनी
वारा—	mas.	बँट-बँटवारा ।
आवट—		सज-सजावट, दिखावट, बुनावट with nouns आम-अमावट ।

हट— fem. चिल्ला—चिल्लाहट, गुर्रा—गुर्राहट
with adjective, कड़ुआ—कड़ुआहट, कड़वाहट

पन— mas. with nouns बच्चा—बचपन, लड़का—लड़कपन

For the purpose of adding many suffixes, the last consonant is taken into consideration because in Hindī the inherent अ in the last letter is not pronounced.

स— fem. मीठा-मिठास, खट्टा-खटास

N. B. Note the changes in the initial vowel. Either the initial vowel assumes its guṇa form, or the guṇa vowel or long vowel assumes its short form.

The following suffixes may be called 'instrumental suffixes' as they form instruments or things by which some work is done.

आ —ठेल—ठेला, झूल—झूला

ई— रेतना - रेती (रेत्+ई)

औटी—कसना —कसौटी (कस् + औटी)

ऊ—झाड़ना - झाड़ू (झाड़् + ऊ)

न—झाड़-झाड़न

ना— (mas.) बेलना, ढकना, घोटना, छन्ना (छनना), झरना, पोतना, पोंछना

नी— (fem.) बेलनी, ढकनी, घोटनी

N. B. Mark that when बेलना, घोटना etc. indicate an instrument, the initial ए and ओ are not fully pronounced. This difference in pronunciation is necessary to indicate its difference with verbs.

नी— कतरनी, मथानी, सुमिरनी, धौंकनी, कब्रखोदनी, बहरनी, नहरनी (*nail-clipper*)

Suffixes forming adjectives.

The following suffixes are added to roots or nouns to form adjectives :

आऊ, आक, आका, आड़ी, आलू, इया, इयल, ईला, ऊ, एला, ऐला, औड़, अक्कड़, आवन, आवना, वन्त, दार, सार, हार, हारा ।

आऊ— टिक —टिकाऊ (टिक् + आऊ), दिखाऊ, बिकाऊ, चलाऊ ।

आक—चालाक

आका—लड़्—लड़ाका

आड़ी—खेल्—खेलाड़ी, अनाड़ी

आरी—हत्यारी

आलू – झगड़—झगड़ालू

इया – बढ़ – बढ़िया, घटिया, रसिया, दुखिया, कनौजिया

इयल – सड़ – सड़ियल, अड़ियल, लतियल, मरियल, डढ़ियल

ई—ऊनी, सूती, रेशमी, देशी

ईला सज—सजीला, नकीला, लचकीला, कँटीला

उआ – बाजार, गेरु – गेरुआ

ऊ बाजारु (बाजार्+ऊ)। खाऊ (खा + ऊ), उड़ाऊ, दिखाऊ।

(In words, with inherent अ not pronounced, ऊ is added to the last letter which is treated as a consonant, but in verbal roots ending in आ—ऊ comes after the last vowel.)

एरा (एरी)—बहुत–बहुतेरा, घन—घनेरा, मामा—ममेरा

एला (एली) – सौत – सौतेला, एक – अकेला, मूँछ – मुछैला

ओड हँस – हँसोड़

अक्कड़— भूल – भुलक्कड़, कुदक्कड़, पियक्कड़

आवन, आवना – सुहावन, लुभावन; सुहावना, लुभावना

वन्त — धनवन्त, गुनवन्त, शीलवन्त

वन्ती— रसवन्ती, गुनवन्ती, कुलवन्ती

सार — मिलनसार

हार — हारा, सिरजनहार, होनहार, रोवनहारा

हा — कटहा, मरकटहा, भुतहा

वाँ — ढलवाँ, कटवाँ

आ — भूख—भूखा, प्यार—प्यारा, मैल—मैला, खार—खारा

ई — भूखी, प्यारी, मैली, खारी

ला — पीछे—पिछला, आगे–अगला, धुँध—धुंधला

ली — माँझ—मँझली

हरा — सोना—सुनहरा, इकहरा

हला — सुनहला, रुपहला

Agentative Suffixes

आर—सोना—सोनार (सुनार), लोहा—लोहार (लुहार)

आरा—बनिज—बनिजारा (बनजारा), घास—घसियारा

आलू—झगड़ा—झगड़ालू, लाज—लजालू

इया—जड़्—जड़िया, गढ़्—गढ़िया, धुन्—धुनिया, आढ़त—आढ़तिया

ई — तमोल (Skt. Tambūl)—तमोली, माला—माली

एरा— साँप—सँपेरा, काँस—कँसेरा,

एरी— पान—पनेरी, पूजा—पुजेरी

ऐया—बच्—बचैया, गा—गवैया, खा—खवैया

After vowel-ending roots, व comes in, before this suffix is added.

वार—घाट—घटवार, रख—रखवार

वाल—कोठी - कोठीवाल

वाला—बोलना—बोलनेवाला, खाना—खानेवाला, पैसा—पैसेवाला, रुपया—रुपयेवाला, चाँदी—चाँदीवाला, धोती—धोतीवाला

Diminutive Suffixes

ओला—खाट—खटोला, साँप—सँपोला

इया—खाट-खटिया, लोटा—लुटिया, डिब्बा—डिबिया, आँख—अँखिया, फोड़ा—फुड़िया

ई—डिब्बा—डिब्बी, (also डब्बा—डब्बी) पिटारा—पिटारी, चिट्ठा—चिट्ठी, रस्सा—रस्सी, गट्ठर - गठरी, डाला— डाली, कड़ाह—कड़ाही

री—छाता—छतरी

ली—टीका—टिकुली, सूप—सुपली, डफ—डफली

ड़ी—आँत—अँतड़ी, पाग—पगड़ी, पंख—पंखड़ी

टी—बहू—बहूटी।

Suffixes forming feminine from masculine

ई—लड़का-लड़की, बेटा-बेटी, चींटा-चींटी, बंदर-बँदरी, मेढक-मेढकी

(last आ is changed to ई)

काका-काकी, दादा-दादी, नाना-नानी, जीजा-जीजी

इया—कुत्ता-कुतिया, बाछा-बछिया, बेटा-बिटिया

बुड्ढ-बुढ़िया (also बुड्ढी)

इन—सुनार-सुनारिन, अहीर-अहिरिन, धोबी-धोबिन, बाघ-बाघिन, कुजड़ा-कुजड़िन, सांप-सांपिन, तेली-तेलिन

आइन—This suffix is added generally to caste surnames.

पाँड़े-पँड़ाइन, दुबे-दुबाइन, चौबे-चौबाइन, ठाकुर-ठकुराइन

आनी—सेठ-सेठानी, देवर-देवरानी, मेहतर-मेहतरानी, चौधरी-चौधरानी, नौकर-नौकरानी, जेठ-जेठानी

Sometimes the same word has two forms one with आइन and another with आनी.

ठकुराइन, ठकुरानी; चौधराइन, चौधरानी,

नी—ऊँट-ऊँटनी, हाथी, हथिनी, मोर-मोरनी

Urdū suffixes

The following Urdū suffixes are formed in common Urdū words.

आना— It forms adjectives.

साल-सालाना, मर्द-मर्दाना, जन-जनाना

ई— It is added to adjectives generally and forms few abstract nouns.

दोस्त-दोस्ती, खुशी, नाराज़-नाराज़ी, नेक-नेकी

It also forms adjectives.

ईरान-ईरानी, ख़ून-ख़ूनी, ख़ाक-ख़ाकी

ईन— It forms adjectives.

शौक़-शौक़ीन, नमक-नमकीन

ईना— It forms adjective and nouns.

माह्-महीना, पश्म-पश्मीना

कार— It is an agentive suffix.

बद-बदकार, पेश-पेशकार, सलाह्-सलाह्कार

गर— It is an agentive suffix.

सौदा-सौदागर, कार-कारीगर, कलई-कलईगर

गार— It is an agentive suffix.

मदद-मददगार, गुनाह्-गुनह्गार

चा— It is a diminutive suffix.

बाग-बागीचा, देग-देगचा, चम-चमचा

दान— It means 'holder or container.'

कलम-कलमदान, इत्र-इत्रदान

दार— It forms agentives and adjectives.

जमीन-जमीनदार, हवा-हवादार, माल-मालदार, फौज-फौजदार

बान— It is an agentive suffix.

बाग-बागवान, दर-दरवान

मेहर-मेहरबान, मेज-मेजवान

नाक— It forms adjectives.

दर्द-दर्दनाक, शर्म-शर्मनाक, खतरा-खतरनाक, ख़ौफ़-ख़ौफ़नाक

नामा— It forms nouns, meaning a letter or deed.

इकरार-इकरारनामा, मुख़्तार-मुख़्तारनामा

आवर— It forms adjectives.

जोर-जोरावर, दस्त-दस्तावर

वर— Agentive जान-जानवर (also used as a noun)

ताकत-ताकतवर

ज़ादा— It means *'born of'*.

शाह-शाहज़ादा, हराम-हरामज़ादा

खोर— It means *'one who eats'*.

हराम-हरामखोर, सूद-सूदखोर

नवीस—It means *'writer of.'*

अरज़ीनवीस, चिट-चिटनवीस

नशीन—It means *'one who sits'*.

तख्त-तख्तनशीन, परदा-परदानशीन

पोश— It means *'one who wears'*, *'one which covers'*.

सफ़ेद-सफ़ेदपोश, सर-सरपोश

साज़— It means *'maker of.'*

जाल-जालसाज़, जीन-जीनसाज़

बाज़— It means *'player of* or *'addicted to'*.

नशा-नशेबाज़, दगा-दगाबाज़

बीन— It means *'seer'*.

तमाशा-तमाशबीन, दूर-दूरबीन

आबाद—It means *'settlement'* and is generally added to cities or places named after some king.

हैदर-हैदराबाद, औरंग-औरंगाबाद

इलाही-इलाहाबाद, अलाहाबाद, अहमद-अहमदाबाद

शाह-शाहाबाद, फर्रुख-फर्रुखाबाद

गाह— It means *'place'*.

दर-दरगाह, चरा-चरागाह, बंदर-बंदरगाह

स्तान, (इस्तान)—It means *'land'* or *'place'*.

तुर्की-तुर्किस्तान, हिन्दू-हिन्दुस्तान

क़ब्र-क़ब्रिस्तान, पाक-पाकिस्तान

आनी—(Arabic)—It forms abstract nouns.

जिस्म-जिस्मानी, रूह-रूहानी

इयत— (Arabic)—It forms abstract nouns.

इंसान-इंसानियत

ई— (Arabic)—It means *possessing the quality of*

इल्म-इल्मी, इंसान-इंसानी

ची— (Arabic)—It means *one who deals in* or *works on.*

तबला-तबलची, मशाल-मशालची

In Hindī all words of Persian, Arabic or Turkish origin are generally called 'Urdu words'.

CHAPTER XVIII

Sandhi

It is a technical term of Sanskṛt grammar, which denotes the euphonic combination of concurrent letters. As thousands of words have come down in Hindī from Sanskṛt and as the technical terms in all branches of learning have been and are being coined from roots and words of that basic language, Sandhi rules assume great importance.

Rules of Sanskṛt grammar apply to Sanskṛt words which are in use in Hindī. In Hindī (Tadbhava and words of non-Sanskṛt origin) words also, analogical rules of Sandhi are observed. Often grammarians only deal with Sanskṛt rules and rules governing genuine Hindī words are not explained. Important Sanskṛt rules are given before Hindī rules are discussed.

Guṇa and Vṛddhi (गुण और वृद्धि)

Guṇa form is arrived by prefixing अ, and Vṛddhi forms by prefixing आ, to vowels अ, इ, उ and ऋ. The following table is useful to the reader :—

Short vowel	Long vowel	Guṇa form	Vṛddhi form	Cognate vowels
अ	आ	अ	आ	
इ	ई	ए	ऐ	य
उ	ऊ	ओ	औ	व
ऋ	ऋ	अर्	आर्	र

For the purpose of Sandhi, it is necessary to know the part of vocal organ, by which a vowel or a consonant is pronounced. Vowels or consonants pronounced from the same vocal organs are called 'similar' (Savarṇa) and those pronounced from different places are called 'dissimilar (asavarṇa). Thus all dentals or palatals are similar to each other.

Sandhi of vowels (स्वर सन्धि)

1. When a vowel अ, इ, उ, short or long, is followed by the same vowel, short or long, the substitute for both is the same long vowel.

अ + अ अ + आ आ + अ आ + आ	आ	कोण + अर्क = कोणार्क परम + आत्मा = परमात्मा विद्या + अभ्यास = विद्याभ्यास महा + आत्मा = महात्मा
इ + इ इ + ई ई + इ ई + ई	ई	रवि + इन्द्र = रवीन्द्र मुनि + ईश = मुनीश अवनी + इन्द्र = अवनीन्द्र नदी + ईश = नदीश
उ + उ उ + ऊ ऊ + उ ऊ + ऊ	ऊ	सु + उक्ति = सूक्ति लघु + ऊर्मि = लघूर्मि वधू + उत्सव = वधूत्सव भू + ऊर्द्ध = भूर्द्ध

If अ or आ is followed इ or उ short or long or ऋ substitute for both is the corresponding गुण form.

अ + इ अ + ई आ + इ आ + ई	ए	सुर + इन्द्र = सुरेन्द्र नर + ईश = नरेश महा + इन्द्र = महेन्द्र महा + ईश = महेश
अ + उ अ + ऊ आ + उ आ + ऊ	ओ	पुरुष + उत्तम = पुरुषोत्तम नव + ऊढ़ा = नवोढ़ा यथा + उचित = यथोचित महा + ऊर्मि = महोर्मि
अ + ऋ आ + ऋ	अर्	देव + ऋषि = देवर्षि महा + ऋषि = महर्षि

If इ, उ. ऋ short or long, is followed by a dissimilar vowel, the substitute is य, व, र.

इ + अ = य्	यदि + अपि = यद्यपि
इ + आ = या	इति + आदि = इत्यादि
ई + अ = य	नदी + अम्बु = नद्यम्बु
ई + आ = या	देवी + आगम = देव्यागम
इ + उ = यु	प्रति + उत्तर = प्रत्युत्तर
इ + ऊ = यू	नि + ऊन = न्यून
ई + उ = यु	सखी + उचित = सख्युचित
ई + ऊ = यू	नदी + ऊर्मि = नद्यूर्मि
इ + ए = ये	प्रति + एक = प्रत्येक
इ + ऐ = यै	मति + ऐक्य = मत्यैक्य
ई + ए = ये	नदी + एक = नद्येक
ई + ऐ = यै	देवी + ऐश्वर्य = देव्यैश्वर्य
उ + अ = व	मनु + अन्तर = मन्वन्तर
उ + आ = वा	सु + आगत = स्वागत
ऊ + अ = व	वधू + अंश = वध्वंश
ऊ + आ = वा	वधू + आगमन = वध्वागमन
उ + ए = ए	अनु + एषण = अन्वेषण
ऋ + अ = र्	पितृ + अनुमति = पित्रनुमति
ऋ + आ = रा	पितृ + आज्ञा = पित्राज्ञा
ऋ + इ = री	नेतृ + ई = नेत्री

When ए, ऐ, ओ, औ is followed by any dissimilar vowel, it becomes अय् , आय् , अव् , आव् respectively.

ए + अ = अय्	ने + अन = नयन
ऐ + अ = आय्	गै + अक = गायक
ओ + अ = अव्	पो + अक = पावक
औ + अ = आव्	पौ + अन = पावन
औ + इ = आवि	नौ + इक = नाविक

When अ, आ, is followed by ए, ऐ it is changed to ऐ and when followed by ओ, औ it is changed to औ। एक + एक = एकैक,

सदा + एव = सदैव, मत + ऐक्य = मतैक्य, जल + ओघ = जलौघ, महा + औषध = महौषध ।

N. B. In my opinion in Hindī, all Sandhi rules of Sanskṛt are not neecssary to be adopted. Sandhi should be considered only when two words coalesing together, have independent existence as words in Hindī.

Thus Sandhi between ने+अन, पो+अक etc. should not come in the domain of Hindī, as ने, पो, अन and अक have no independent existence as words in Hindī. No Hindī dictionary would give place to ने, पो, गे etc. in it. Illustrations of many rules are difficult to find even in Modern Hindī, what to speak of classical Hindī literature. It is too much to ask a Hindī student to disjoin the Sandhi in जय, स्तव, रव, etc., which should be studied in Sanskṛt grammar.

In my humble opinion, Sandhi of ऋ+ऋ is also alien to Hindī as words ending in ऋ are not adopted in Hindī. Hindī has taken from Sanskṛt पिता, माता, नेता, जेता etc. and not पितृ, मातृ, जेतृ. So a Hindī student should not reasonably be expected to disjoin Sandhis of नेत्री, पित्राज्ञा. We have given some such Sandhis only, because there is a tradition to deal them in popular Hindī grammars. Illustrations of many rules given above are often not met with.

The table given below would show the effect of Sandhi on vowels.

अ, आ	followed by	अ, आ—	is changed to	आ
ई, ई	,,	ई, ई	,,	ई
उ, ऊ	,,	उ, ऊ	,,	ऊ
ऋ	,,	ऋ	,,	ॠ
अ	,,	इ	,,	ए
अ	,,	उ	,,	ओ
अ	,,	ऋ	,,	अर्
अ	,,	ए, ऐ	,,	ऐ
अ	,,	ओ, औ	,,	औ

इ, ई	followed by a dissimilar vowel is changed to		य
उ, ऊ	,,	,,	व
ऋ	,,	,,	र
ए	,,	,,	अय्
ऐ	,,	,,	आय्
ओ	,,	,,	अव्
औ	,,	,,	आव्

Sandhi of Consonants

In Sandhi of consonants, the last consonant of the first word is assimilated to the first letter, vowel or consonant of the second word. e. g. सत्+जन=सज्जन, दिक्+अम्बर=दिगम्बर

1. The first letter of a class changes to the third letter of its own class, if it is followed by any vowel or third letter of a class.

क्	-	ग्	वाक्+ईश=वागीश
च्	-	ज्	अच्+अन्त=अजन्त
ट्	-	ड्	षट्+दर्शन=षड्दर्शन
त्	-	द्	जगत्+ईश=जगदीश
प्	-	ब	अप्+ज=अब्ज

2. क् च् ट् त् प् changes to a nasal of its class, if followed by a nasal.

क्	-	ङ	वाक्मय=वाङ्मय
च्	-	ञ्	याच्+ना=याच्ञा
ट्	-	ण्	षट्मास=षण्मास
त्	-	न्	जगत्नाथ=जगन्नाथ
प्	-	म्	अप्मय=अम्मय (rarely used)

3. Change of त् at the end of the first word.

त् changes to द् if followed by गध, दध, बभ, य, र, व or a vowel.

त्ग	–	द्	सत्गुरु	=	सद्गुरु
त्घ	–	द्	उत्घाटन	=	उद्घाटन
त्ध	–	द्	सत्धर्म	=	सद्धर्म
त्भ	–	भ्	सत्भाव	=	सद्भाव
त्य	–	द्	उत्योग	=	उद्योग
त्र	–	द्	तत्रूप	=	तद्रूप

त् followed by च्, छ् changes to च्–उत् चारण=उच्चारण उत्छेद=उच्छेद

by ज् to ज्-सत्जन=सज्जन

by ल् to ल्-तत्लीन=तल्लीन

If त् is followed by ह् then त् changes to द् and ह् to क्

उत्	+	हार	=	उद्	+	धार	=	उद्धार
तत्	+	हित	=	तद्	+	धित	=	तद्धित

If त् is followed by श् then त् changes to च् and श् to छ्

उत्	+	शिष्ट	=	उच्	+	छिष्ट	=	उच्छिष्ट
उत्	+	श्वास	=	उच्	+	छ्वास	=	उच्छ्वास

The following rules are also observed :

(a) छ coming after a vowel becomes च्छ, परि+छेद=परिच्छेद, वि+छेद=विच्छेद ।

(b) If म् at the end of a word is followed by a consonant of the five classes, it changes to the nasal of its class or to Anusvār optionally but if it is followed by a semi-vowel (अन्तःस्थ) or sibilants (श ष स ह), it is necessarily changed to anusvār.

सम् + कल्प-सङ्कल्प संकल्प

सम् + तोष-सन्तोष संतोष

but सम्+वत्=संवत्, सम्+योग=संयोग

(c) If ष् is followed by त् and थ् then त् and थ् become ट् and ठ् respectively.

आकृष् + त = आकृष्ट

पृष् + थ = पृष्ठ

(d) If ज् is followed by न, न् becomes ञ्

यज् + न = यज् + ञ = यज्ञ

(e) स् and र् at the end of a word is changed to Visarga (:) if क्, ख्, प फ् श् ष् स्, come there after

रजस्कण – रजःकण

मनस्खेद – मनःखेद

अधस्पतन – अधःपतन

तपस्फल – तपःफल

(2) If स् at the end of a word is followed by च or छ it changes to श्

तपस्+चर्या = तपश्चर्या

निस् + छल = निश्छल

(3) If अस् is followed by अ or a voiced consonant it changes to ओ

मनस् + अनुकूल = मनोअनुकूल—मनोनुकूल

सरस् + ज = सरोज

मनस् + ज = मनोज

4. If स् comes after a vowel other than अ or आ and is also followed by a vowel or by a voiced consonant, it changes to र् आयुस्वेद-आयुर्वेद.

If स् comes after a vowel other than अ or आ and is followed by क, ख, प, फ it changes to ष.

निस्काम = निष्काम, निस्फल = निष्फल. निस्पक्ष = निष्पक्ष

N. B. Many rules of consonantal Sandhi are only met in Sanskṛt. So it is not necessary for an average reader to know all the intricate rules in detail.

Visarga Sandhi

1. After Visarga, if च or छ comes, it changes to श्, त, थ to स् and ट् ठ् to ष्.

निःचल = निश्चल, मनःताप = मनस्ताप, धनुःटंकार = धनुष्टंकार

2. If श ष or स् comes after Visarga, it is either not changed or is changed to the letter coming after it.

निःसन्देह = निःसन्देह-निस्सन्देह

निःसृत = निःसृत-निस्सृत

निःसार = निःसार-निस्सार

3. If अ comes before Visarga and after it the third, fourth and fifth letter of a class, a semi-vowel or ह comes, the Visarga is substituted by ओ.

यशःदा = यशोदा, मनःहर = मनोहर, तपःभूमि = तपोभूमि, वयःवृद्ध = वयोवृद्ध, पयःधि = पयोधि, अधःगति = अधोगति

4. If a vowel other than अ comes before Visarga and the third, fourth, fifth letter of a class, a semivowel or ह comes after it, the Visarga is changed to र्.

निःआधार = निर्आधार = निराधार

आशीःवाद = आशीर्वाद = आशीर्वाद

5. If र comes after र्, then र् is deleted and the preceding vowel is lengthened.

निर्रोग-नीरोग, निर्रस-नीरस

If अ comes before Visarga which is followed by a vowel other than अ, the Visarga disappears : अतःएव-अतएव

Sandhi in Hindī words

If we study the formation of genuine Hindī words, we observe the application of several Sandhi rules, which are based on sound phonetic principles.

Thus पढ़े is formed by adding ए to root पढ़्, सुने by adding ए to सुन् and so on.

But in root ending in long vowels like खा, जा, गा etc. in my opinion य् is added before ए is joined खाय्+ए=खाये, जाय्+ए=जाये, गाय्+ए=गाये, बोय्+ए=बोये.

These forms are sanctioned by usage and tradition of spelling of former literary Avadhī and Brajbhāsā forms. खाय, जाय, बोय, सुनाय, दिखाय etc. may be quoted. However some writers are of opinion that खाए, जाए, गाए, बोए are the correct forms and they would say that ए simply comes after the long-vowel roots in Hindī. I am in favour of taking य् in such formations and ए in mātrā form is joined to the consonant. There are scholars who say that Hindī has no consonantal root and पढ़, सुन etc. should be treated as roots and so पढ़े is पढ़+ए but this is not in accordance with rules of Sandhi. अ+ए is substituted by ऐ and not ए e g. एक+एक=एकैक. So पढ़+ए may become पढ़ै not पढ़े. So in पढ़े, सुने etc. the vowel ए is simply added to the previous consonant ढ़् or न् in पढ़् or सुन्. When a vowel is added to a consonant in Hindī it assumes the *Mātrā* form. Two vowels, if they come near each other should combine. If you say that ए comes after खा then two vowels should combine ख्+आ+ए but this does not happen in Hindī. So it is better to write खाये (ख+आ+य्+ए) and not खाए*.)

N. B. I think that जाये and खाये forms should be preferred because they show the existence of य् clearly.

---

* This discussion is for mature students of Hindī grammar and is a subject of controversy even among scholars in Hindī.

The formation of सुना, पढ़ा, कहा is like this :

सुन् + आ, पढ़् + आ, कह् + आ

Those who are of opinion that सुन, पढ़ and कह are roots would say that there is Sandhi here of अ + अ = आ

सुन + आ = सुना, पढ़ + आ = पढ़ा, कह + आ = कहा

As Sandhi is phonetic coalesence, in सुन, पढ़ and कह the inherent अ is not pronounced.

Dropping of one consonant when followed by the same consonant.

यही, वही—यह + ही य् + अ + ह् (अ) + ह् + ई = ह् is followed by ह् as अ of first ह is inherent. Therefore the first ह् is dropped. य् + अ + ह् + ई = यही

Similarly we have वह + ही = वही

यहीं = यहाँ + ही वहीं = वहाँ + ही	In these two words हाँ is doppped. The influence of nasalization is seen in ही which becomes हीं,
कभी जभी तभी सभी	They are formed as shown here कब् + ह् + ई, जब् + ह् + ई, तब् + ह् + ई, सब् + ह् + ई. There is inherent अ in कब, जब, तब, सब-ब् + ह् = भ् Therefore कभ् + ई, जभ् + ई, तभ् + ई, सभ् + ई = कभी, जभी तभी, सभी ।

पढ़ो, करो, सुनो :—

Here ओ is the suffix which is added to पढ़्, कर् and सुन्

पढ़ो = पढ़् + ओ, करो = कर् + ओ, सुनो = सुन् + ओ, खा + ओ = खाओ, सो + ओ = सोओ (optionally written as सोवो)

पीओ (पीयो), सीओ (सीओ) पिओ, सिओ which become पियो, सियो (letter forms are preferred)

After roots ending in ओ, व् comes between the root and suffix. After roots ending in ई, य् come between the root and suffix and the intial vowel is shortened. पी—पिया, पिये, पियो ।

Sandhi in some compound words.

हरेक, कुछेक—

In these words we find Sandhi between हर + एक and कुछ+एक The inherent अ in हर and कुछ is not pronounced and so र and छ may be treated as consonants.

The general rule of Hindī Sandhis that the initial vowel of the suffix or a word merges with the last vowel of a root or the last consonant seems to be applicable here also.

N. B. Here some important characteristics only of Hindī Sandhi are given.

CHAPTER XIX.

Samāsa (Compound words.)

The formation of compound words is governed by certain definite rules and expounding of these compound words (Samāsa) helps in understanding their meaning. A large number of compound words in Hindī come down from Sanskṛt and are governed by rules of Sanskṛt grammar. However there are pure Hindī compound words also, in which both the component parts are Hindī tadbhava words. A few compounds may be treated as 'hybrid compounds,' in which one component word is Hindī and the other a foreign word. There are some pure compounds of Urdū or English words.

Sanskṛt compounds:—राजकुमार, राष्ट्रपति, सभापति, नरेश, यथाशक्ति, नीलकमल, प्रतिदिन, रविवार etc.

Hindī compounds :—कठघरा, गोजई, हथकड़ी, अधमरा, अधपका फुलवारी, पतझड़, चिड़ीमार, अमचूर, गुड़म्बा, दुधमुँहा ।

Urdū compounds :—बेशक, हररोज, राहखर्च, बंदरगाह, ताजमहल, सौदागर, नालायक, गैरहाजिर, खुशबू ।

English compounds :—स्टेशनमास्टर, हेडमास्टर, हाईकोर्ट, चेयरमैन ।

Hybrid compounds :—बेकाम, बेसुरा (बे—Urdū prefix; काम Hindī) डिगरीदार—'Degree' English, दार Urdū. जिलाधीश-जिला Urdū अधीश Sanskṛt जेबघड़ी-जेब Urdū घड़ी Hindī. सितार-सि (Urdū-three) तार Hindī.

The Indian grammarians recognise four main kinds of samās as e. g. Avyayībhāva, Tatpurusa, Dvandva and Bahuvrīhi. This classification is based on the position, importance and nature of the component words. In Hindī, generally, compound of two words only are in use. In Sanskṛt, however a Samāsa may combine with another word or with another Samāsa. If the first word is important it is Avyavībhava; if the second is important it is Tatpuruṣa, if both are important it is Dvandva and if neither of the two is important and the whole compound refers to some other person, it is Bahuvrīhi.

If the first member is a numeral, the Samāsa is called Dvigu, as त्रिकोण *'triangle'*. If the first member is a prefix, it is called *prādi* (प्रादि तत्पुरुष). If the first member is अ or अन् it is called नञ् nañ. If the relationship between the two words is that of an adjective and substantive (विशेष्य) or if both are adjectives, the compound is called Karmadhāraya. In a Tatpuruṣa compound, the relation subsisting between the two members is that which may be properly expressed by the various cases.

After these introductory remarks it is necessary to deal with each kind of compound in some detail.

Avyayībhāva—(Adverbial compounds)

In such a compound the first member is an Avyaya (Indeclinable) यथाशक्ति *as far as one can* यथासंभव *as far as possible* प्रत्यक्ष *before one's eye.*

Hindī compounds formed by repeating the same words (nouns) are also classed under this head.

रातों रात, हाथों हाथ ।

Tatpuruṣa—(Determinative compounds)

In such a compound, the relationship subsisting between the two members is expressed by different cases, like the Accusative (कर्म), the Instrumental (करण) the Dative (सम्प्रदान), the Ablative (अपादान) and the Genitive (सम्बन्ध) and the locative (अधिकरण). In such compounds the case-signs are dropped, and the first member in some form qualifies the second member which is important,

It has six varieties according to the six cases referred to above.

Accusative, omission of को—स्वर्गप्राप्त (स्वर्ग को प्राप्त) *'heaven-reached'*
पिछलगा (पीछे को लगा) *'a follower'*

Instrumental	से—	कंटकाकीर्ण (कंटक से आकीर्ण) *'Thorn-ful'*
Dative	के लिये—	बलिपशु (बलि के लिये पशु) *'sacrificial animal'*
		रसोई घर (रसोई के लिये घर) *'kitchen'*
Ablative	से—	पदच्युत (पद से च्युत) *'fallen from post'*
		देशनिकाला (देश से निकाला) *'externed'*
Genitive	का—	राजपुत्र (राजा का पुत्र) *'prince'*
		डाकघर (डाक का घर) *'post office'*
Locative	में, पर—	आनन्दमग्न (आनन्द में मग्न) *'immersed in pleasure'*
		घुड़सवार— (घोड़े पर सवार) *'mounted on horse'*

A compound may be expounded in different ways. If रसोईघर is expounded. —as रसोई का घर it will be 'genitive determinative' (सम्बन्ध तत्पुरुष) but if expounded as रसोई के लिए घर it is dative determinative. (सम्प्रदान तत्पुरुष)' If घुड़सवार is expounded as घोड़े का सवार it is 'genitive determinative, if it is expounded as घोड़े पर सवार it is Locative determinative अधिकरण तत्पुरुष, if it is expounded as घोड़े पर सवार है, जो— *a horse-rider*, it is Bahuvrīhi. In Hindī expounding of Samāsa (समास-विग्रह) is not in a particular set form, it may be variously expounded.

Tatpuruṣa has another form in which one member is in apposition to the other. In a compound word पुरुषसिंह both members are in apposition to each other. Such a compound is called Karmadhāraya also. Thus Tatpuruṣa has two forms, one inflexional and the other appositional (समानाधिकरण). In Appositional compounds both members have same case signs. Karmadhāraya is a sub-class of Tatpuruṣa.

Karmdhāraya—In such a compound either member may be an adjective or both may be adjectives.

शुभागमन—	'welcome'	शुभ	adj. — first member.
पुरुषोत्तम—	'nobleman'	उत्तम	adj. —second member.
शीतोष्ण—	'cold-hot'	शीत and उष्ण both adj.	

रक्त कमल— red lotus, मंदबुद्धि dull in intelligence
बदबू— bad smell.

A Karmadhāraya may also denote 'similarity' between the two members.

चन्द्रमुख— 'moon-face' — the second member is compared with the first member.

चरण-कमल — 'lotus-feet' — the first is compared with the second.

Dvigu —When the first member of a compound is numeral it is called Dvigu.

नवरत्न— nine jewels पंचपात्र 'five utensils' used specially in 'Puja', (तिमंजिला) three-storeyed, चौमुहानी a place where four roads meet, छमाही six-monthly.

Bahuvrīhi :—In this compound reference is to something other than which is actually expressed by the component words of the compound. The English compounds 'good-natured' 'ill-tempered' 'narrow-minded' are of this type. A large number of Bahuvrīhi compound, are taken from Sanskṛt. In Karmadhāraya, the sense is complete in the compound but in Bahuvrīhi it is not the case, here the whole compound is generally an adjective. Many Bahuvrihi samāsas have fixed meaning by tradition.

लम्बोदर-लम्ब+उदर— 'long belley' but it particularly refers to a God Gaṇeśa, who is pot-bellied.

चक्रपाणि— 'wheel-hand', but it refers to a god Viṣṇu, having a wheel in his hand.

दशानन— 'Ten-faced' —refers to Rāvaṇa, who had ten mouths.

पंकज— Born of 'mud' — 'lotus' — Many things may come out of mud, but it refers to lotus only.

अनन्त—*'endless'* or *infinite*— it refers to God who is infinite.

Tadbhava Bahuvrīhi compounds are few in number,

हँसमुख—*'Smiling-face.'*–- *a man having a smiling face.*

दुधमुँहा—*'milk-mouthed'*— *a child feeding on mother's milk.*

टुटपुँजिया— literally *'broken capitalist'* - *a businessman with a small capital.*

नौलखा— *'of nine lakhs.'* — *a thing made of nine lakhs.*

द्वन्द्व— **(Copulative compound.)**

In this form of compound two words combine but the copula (और) is absent. सीताराम, राजारानी, लोटाडोरी · Sometimes words of opposite meaning are also like-wise compounded. हानि-लाभ *'profit-loss'* जीवन-मरण *life and death.*

हाथपैर, रोटीदाल, चावलदाल, साग-सत्तू, काम-काज— are other examples of this compound in Hindī.

Sometimes verbs and adverbs also combine and और omitted. धीरे-धीरे, उठते-बैठते, चलना-फिरना, उठना-गिरना ।

The subject of Sāmāsa is very exhaustively treated in Sanskṛt grammars. There are various sub-classes and forms of compounds, which are not necessary for a beginner to learn.

Besides the above important classes of compounds the following may also be noted.

Negative compounds. नञ् समास

Such compounds begin with अ before a Skt. word having an initial consonant and with अन् before a word having an initial vowel. This अन् may be compared with *'un'* in 'unkind' 'unmindful' etc. in English.

अपार, असार, अगाध, अचल, अथक— etc.

अनन्त, अनादि, अनुदार, अनेक— etc.

In Hindī अन also comes before a word beginning with a consonant अनजान, अनपढ़, अनगिनत, अनहोनी ।

Upapada compounds उपपद

When the second member is such a word, which cannot be used independently, and only comes as the second mem ber in a compound, it is called Upapada Samāsa e.g. कार, स्थ, घ्न, etc.

ग्रन्थकार *'author'* कुम्भकार *'potter'* मध्यस्थ *'arbitrator'*,

गृहस्थ *'a householder'* कृतघ्न *'ungrateful'* शत्रुघ्न *'enemy-killer'* सौदागर *a trader* जादूगर *'a magician'* वान—गाड़ीवान *'a bullock-cart, driver* or *a carriage-driver'*.

Here words like कार, स्थ, घ्न, गर, बान, are not used separately. वाला is also such a word— पानीवाला *a water man*, चाँदीवाला *one who deals in silver*, सोनेवाला *one who sleeps* कमाने वाला *one who earns*.

Prādi प्रादि तत्पुरुष

According to Sanskṛt grammarians, compound words formed by prefixes is called Prādi compounds.

प्रयोग, उपयोग, वियोग, नियोग, आहार, विहार, संहार, विचार, आचार, दुराचार, नियम — are Prādi compounds. In Hindī निडर, निकम्मा, निलज are its examples.

Madhyampadalopi Samasa मध्यमपदलोपी समास

Here the case-sign of the first member is not dropped. Such compounds have also come down in Hindī from Sanskṛt.

सरसिज *lotus* pond-born. मनसिज *Cupid.* (mind-born) युधिष्ठिर (the name of the eldest brother among Pāṇḍavās) literally *fixed or unnerved in war.*

In the words सरसि, मनसि and युधि the locative case-sign is retained.

In Hindī in case of many compounds, we have to bring some other words to give it a clear meaning so they are also treated as Madhyampadalopī compounds.

पानीपाँडे— means पानी पिलानेवाला पाँडे

दहीबड़ा— बड़ा *a kind of food-preparation prepared in curd.* दही में बना हुआ बड़ा ।

N. B. For a foreign student of Hindī, the subject of samāsa is not of very great importance. So we have not entered into the niceties of distinction drawn by the Indian grammarians.

CHAPTER XX

Punctuation in Hindī

In Hindī all punctuation signs except the full stop sign have been adopted from English. For full stop the traditional sign is (।) a vertical stroke, is still in use.

In poems (॥) two vertical strokes were formerly used to denote the end of a metre or a stanza. But this practice of placing two vertical strokes is being discarded by modern writers.

गुरु पद रज मृदु मंजुल अंजन । नयन अमिअ दृग दोष विभंजन ॥

The following signs taken from English are in common use in Hindī also.

- , Comma.
- ? Note of interrogation.
- ! Note of exclamation.
- — Dash.
- " " Inverted commas.
- ' ' Semi-inverted comma,
- - Hyphen.
- ( ) Bracket.

Of these, the use of comma is not very regular in Hindī. It is however used generally in the following cases :—

(1) When words of the same nature, nouns, pronouns, verbs or adjectives - come together, a comma is used after every such word.

विद्या, विनय, शील और सात्विकता से वे पूर्ण थे ।

मैं, तुम और वे बाजार जा रहे थे ।

चलते, फिरते, उठते, बैठते, सोते, जागते वे बराबर रामनाम लेते थे ।

चलते-फिरते, उठते-बैठते, सोते-जागते, वे बराबर रामनाम लेते थे ।

Here comma is placed after every pair of words.

(2) Comma is used after a noun, when the words coming after it, are in apposition.

दशरथ जो अयोध्या के राजा थे, राम के वन जाते ही मूर्छित हो गये ।

"जो अयोध्या के राजा थे" is in apposition to Daśrath.

(3) When many clauses (generally adverbial) are in a sentence, after every clause.

Mark the use of comma in the following sentence taken from Pratijña, a novel of Premchand.

लोग समझते हैं, मैं आवार हूँ, सिनेमा और थिएटर में प्रमोद के लिये हार्दिक वेदनाओं को भुलाने के लिये जाता हूँ, अपनी अतृप्त अभिलाषाओं को और कैसे शान्त करूँ, दिल की आग को कैसे बुझाऊँ । कभी-कभी जी में आता है, संन्यासी हो जाऊँ और कदाचित् एक दिन यही करना पड़ेगा ।

(4) After any proper noun in the vocative case.

"पूर्णा, तुम जिस संकट में हो, मैं उसे जानता हूं ।"

(5) After हाँ or नहीं in dialogue.

हाँ, इच्छा न होगी, मैंने कह दिया न ।"
कमला—नहीं, शायद कोई जरूरी काम है ।

(6) After pause in poems.*

तीस कोटि सुत, अर्ध नग्न तन,
अन्न वस्त्र पीड़ित अनपढ़ जन,
झाड़्-फूस खर के घर आँगन,

—पंत

(7) In writing several numerals together

३, ४, ८, ६— etc.

---

* N. B. Several modern poets are not using comma after the pause in each line—

(8) When a noun clause is not joined by any conjunctive word.

'प्रेम ईश्वर की प्रेरणा है, उसको स्वीकार करना पाप नहीं, उसका अनादर करना पाप है ।'

Use of Hyphen

-Hyphen is used between two words of same, similar or dis-similar nature. It joins two members of a copulative compound.

सुख-दुःख, दिन-रात, माँ-बाप, भाई-बहन, पूजा-पाठ, धूप-दीप, चलते-फिरते, उठते-बैठते, सोते-जागते, रोते-रोते, करते-धरते, गिरते-पड़ते ।

—**Dash** – Dash is more often used in dramas and novels after the name of a character where his speech begins

चन्द्रगुप्त— चाणक्य—

As regards the use of inverted commas, single or double, it is commonly used to quote any speech or writing. The note of interrogation is used when a question is asked as in English.

तुम कहाँ गये थे ? क्यों जा रहे हो ?

!—**Sign of interjection or exclamation.** Sometimes these signs are used only to express sense of intense surprize, bewilderment or awe. Sometimes Hindi writers use two or three signs !! !!! to express the degree of intensity of feeling.

THE END

Appendix—I Grammatical terms in Hindi.

Grammar.	Vyākaraṇa.	Ablative,	Apādāna.
Language	Bhāṣā	Genitive	Sambandh.
Dialect.	Bolī, upbhāśā.	Possessive.	,,
Sentence	Vākya.	Locative.	Adhikaraṇa.
Word.	Śabda.	Gender.	Linga.
Letter.	Varṇa, Akṣara.	Masculine.	Puṁlinga.
Vowel.	Svara.	Feminine.	Strīlinga.
Consonant.	Vyañjana.	Neuter.	Napunsaka.
		Compound words.	Samāsa.
Semi-vowel.	Antasth.	Indeclinable.	Avyaya.
Sibilant.	ūṣma.	Object.	Karma.
Gutteral.	Kaṇthya.	Primary object.	Mukhya Karma.
Palatal.	Tālavya.	Secondary. ,,	Gauṇa Karma.
Cerebral	Mūrdhaṇya.	Conjunction.	Sanyojak.
Dental.	Dantya.	Interjection.	Vismayādibodhak
Labial.	Oṣṭhya.		
Nasal.	Anunāsik.	Person.	Puruṣa.
Noun.	Sanjña.	First Person.	Prathama Puruṣa.
Proper Noun.	Vyaktivācaka.	Second ,,	Madhyama Puruṣa.
Common ,,	Jātivācak.	Third ,,	Anya Puruṣa.
Concrete ,,	Padārthavācaka.	Prefix.	Upasarga.
Material ,,	Dravyavācaka.	Suffix.	Pratyaya.

Abstract ,,	Bhavavācaka.	Pronunciation.	Uccāraṇa.
Root.	Dhātu.	Accent.	Svarāghāt.
Verb.	Kriyā.	Long.	Dīrgha,
Transitive	Sakarmaka.	Short.	Hrasva.
Intransitive.	Akarmaka.	Pause.	Virām, Yati (in metre)
Causative.	Preraṇārthaka.	Parsing	Padānvaya.
Auxilary.	Sahāyak Kriyā.	Subject.	Uddeśya.
Adverb.	Kriyāviśeṣaṇa	Predicate.	Vidheya,
,, of time.	Kalvācaka.	Voice.	Vācya.
,, of place.	Sthanvācaka.	Active voice.	Kartṛ Vācya
,, of manner.	Rītivācaka.	Passive ,,	Karma ,,
,, of degree.	Parimāṇavācaka.	Derivation.	Vyutpatti
Adjective.	Viśeṣaṇa	Impersonal.	Bhāva vācya.
Pronominal adjective.	Sārvanāmik	Construction.	Prayog,
Numerical.	Sankhyāvācaka.	Analysis.	Vākyaviśleṣaṇa.
Qualitative.	Guṇavacaka.	Aspirated letter	Mahāprāṇa.
Quantitative	Parimāṇavācaka.	Unaspirated.	Alpaprāṇa
Pronoun.	Sarvanām.	Nasal mark.	Anusvār
Demonstrative.	Niścayavācaka.	Semi-nasal mark.	Chandravindu
Indefinite.	Aniścayavācaka.	Personal.	Purusvācaka.
Relative.	Sambandhvācaka.	Interrogative.	Praśnavācak.
Reflexive.	Nijvācaka.	Case.	Kāraka.
Case-Sign.	Vibhakti.	Nominative case.	Kartā kāraka.

Accusative.	Karma.	Instrumental.	Karaṇa.
Dative.	Sampradāna.	Tense.	Kāl.
Present tense.	Vartamān kāl.	Past ,,	Bhut Kāl.
Future ,,	Bhaviṣyat ,,	Present imperfect.	Samānya vartmān.
Present perfect.	Samānya Vartmān. Asanna Bhūt.	Past imperfect.	Purṇa vartamān.
Past perfect.	Pūrṇa Bhut.	Contingent imperfect.	Samānya vartamān.
Contingent perfect.	Samānaya Bhūt.	Presumptive imperfect.	Sandigdha vartamān.
Presumptive perfect.	Sandīgdha Bhūt.	Past contingent imperfect.	Apurṇa sanketārth.
Past contingent perfect.	Pūrṇa Sanketārth.	Indefinite imperfect.	Sāmānya Sanketarth Hetuhetumatbhut.
Indefinite perfect.	Samānya Bhūt.	Contingent future.	Sambhāvya Bhaviṣyat.
Imperative.	Pratyakṣa vidhi, vidhi.	Absolute future.	Sāmānya Bhaviṣyat.

N. B.—Hindī equivalents for preposition, mood and articles are not given, as they are not of any importance in Hindī grammar.

* Hindī grammarians have given different names to these tenses. Here we have given the names of tenses according to Guru.